Snorkeling the Florida Keys

UNIVERSITY PRESS OF FLORIDA

Florida A&M University, Tallahassee
Florida Atlantic University, Boca Raton
Florida Gulf Coast University, Ft. Myers
Florida International University, Miami
Florida State University, Tallahassee
New College of Florida, Sarasota
University of Central Florida, Orlando
University of Florida, Gainesville
University of North Florida, Jacksonville
University of South Florida, Tampa
University of West Florida, Pensacola

Snorkeling the Florida Keys

BRAD BERTELLI

University Press of Florida
Gainesville · Tallahassee · Tampa · Boca Raton
Pensacola · Orlando · Miami · Jacksonville · Ft. Myers · Sarasota

VIVA FLORIDA 500
1513–2013

A Florida Quincentennial Book

18 17 16 15 14 13   6 5 4 3 2 1

Library of Congress Cataloging-in-Publication Data
Bertelli, Brad.
Snorkeling the Florida Keys / Brad Bertelli.
p. cm.
Includes bibliographical references and index.
    Summary: Focuses on 14 segments of the Florida Reef, featuring historically
significant wrecks, lighthouses, state parks, etc. Provides GPS coordinates and
practical travel hints.
ISBN 978-0-8130-4452-1 (alk. paper)
    1. Skin diving—Florida—Florida Keys—Guidebooks. 2. Scuba diving—
Florida—Florida Keys—Guidebooks. 3. Florida Keys (Fla.)—Guidebooks.
4. Global Positioning System. I. Title.
GV838.673.U6B47 2013
797.2'340975941—dc23   2012039461

University Press of Florida
15 Northwest 15th Street
Gainesville, FL 32611-2079
http://www.upf.com

Contents

Introduction. vii

1. Biscayne National Park 1

2. Carysfort Reef 13

3. John D. Pennekamp Coral Reef State Park 25

4. *City of Washington* 35

5. Molasses Reef 44

6. Pickles Reef 51

7. Alligator Reef 60

8. Indian Key 69

9. Coffins Patch Reef 82

10. Sombrero Reef 90

11. Bahia Honda State Park 97

12. Looe Key 107

13. Key West Marine Park 114

14. Dry Tortugas National Park 123

Acknowledgments 134

Photo Credits 135

Bibliography. 137

Index 141

Introduction

> There is no portion of the American coast more dangerous to the
> mariner, or where more property is annually wrecked, than on the
> Florida reef. Its contiguity to the gulf stream, and forming a sort of
> Scylla to that Charybdis, the Bahama islands, are the main causes
> which make it so dangerous to, and so much dreaded by, seamen.
> (Macgregor 1847: 355)

Snorkeling the Florida Keys delivers the necessary directions,
depths, descriptions, habitat identifications, and GPS coordinates
to some of the best snorkeling sites that area has to offer. It then
does something more. While an excellent snorkeling guide, *Snorkeling the Florida Keys* reveals stories of the pirates, shipwrecks,
wars, and hurricanes that have helped to define not only the Florida Reef, but also the Sunshine State's most famous archipelago,
the Florida Keys.

The Atlantic waters separating this island chain from the Bahamas channel the Gulf Stream. Were it not for this current's presence, the Florida Reef would not have formed. The Gulf Stream
distributes nutrient-rich, warm, clear water—the exact combination of environmental factors that catalyze coral growth.

It took a long time—thousands of years—but, slowly, coral after
coral grew until they created the barrier reef system called today
the Florida Reef. It is continental North America's best snorkeling

opportunity. According to the Florida Department of Environmental Protection, the Florida Reef is 358 miles long and stretches along the Atlantic seabed from the St. Lucie Inlet, some 100 miles north of Miami, to the Dry Tortugas, 70 miles southwest of Key West.

It is the third-largest barrier reef system in the world. Only the reef systems off the coasts of Australia and Belize are bigger. Interestingly, the Florida Reef is not a single reef, but rather a collection of a somewhat striated series of 6,000 or so individual reefs. While today they are a playground for snorkelers, fishermen, and divers, they were once feared by sailors. When sailing ships crashed against these reefs, the corals carved up their wooden hulls like stony daggers.

With time, the reefs were tamed by the captains of industry. Maps and charts improved. Day markers and iron-framed lighthouses were erected, standing like scarecrows at the more dangerous banks. Ships, too, switched from sail to more navigationally reliable steam power, and coral reefs came to be recognized as ecological marvels, the rain forests of the sea.

One thing that should be made clear, however, is that coral is neither a plant nor a rock and should never be picked, touched, or manipulated. Coral is a delicate kind of organism. They are respiring animals in the class of jellyfish and sea anemones that begin life as meroplankton. Meroplankton spend the early stages of their life as vagabonds adrift with the ocean currents and tides. As they mature, however, the corals sink and begin to settle upon a suitable substrate.

Individually, corals are referred to as polyps. These polyps look like tiny upside-down jellyfish. The first job a newly settled polyp undertakes is constructing a home. It begins secreting calcium carbonate, which it uses like cement to construct the tiny limestone walls of its house. These homes are generally small, smaller than the pinkish eraser of a number two pencil.

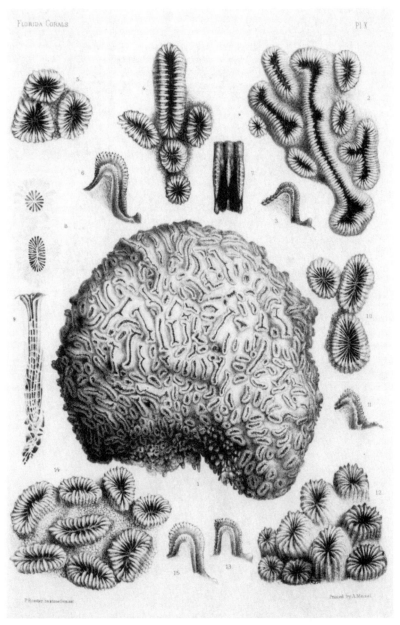

This drawing of a stony coral comes from a report by Louis Agassiz, who conducted one of the first studies of the Florida Reef. Courtesy of NOAA.

Sea fan published in Louis Agassiz's "Report on the Florida Reefs" from Memoirs of the Museum of Comparative Zoology at Harvard College. Courtesy of NOAA.

While the house of a single polyp is no more impressive than a barnacle, events begin to occur that change everything. Another coral floats down from the currents like a snowflake and settles in next door to the original polyp, where it too builds a home. The process repeats over and over, one polyp at a time, for hundreds and thousands of years until an entire reef has been formed.

The polyps join together to create extravagant colonies of impressive design. These designs help to identify different types of corals. For instance, brain coral is so named because the intricately grooved structure the colony creates resembles a human brain. The sea fan, a particularly elegant soft coral, creates a flexible structure similar in appearance to those delicately laced fans once popular in antebellum houses.

There are hundreds and maybe thousands of species and subspecies of coral, and each basically falls into one of two groups, hard and soft. The hard corals are called stony corals, which comprise the backbone of the reef. With names like star, pillar, elkhorn, and staghorn corals, they decorate a reef like the hood ornament on a 1976 Cadillac Coupe de Ville.

The other kind of coral is octocoral; these are the soft corals. Octocorals are flexible and lack the limestone skeletons that stony corals create. Rather, their homes have a woody quality and respond to the push and pull of the currents as a stalk of wheat does to wind. These soft corals have names like slimy sea feathers, sea rods, and sea whips.

One of the most crucial pieces of coral information that needs to be disclosed, however, is that these organisms have one rather significant flaw. In fact, to say that they are slow builders would be an understatement. It can take decades for a coral colony to construct a structure as big as a coconut. The Florida Reef required thousands of years of hard coral labor to form and is thought to be in the neighborhood of 7,000 years old.

The two most common reef structures snorkelers will explore are spur-and-groove reef formations and patch reef formations. Spur-and-groove reefs are one part sand and one part coral. Sandy grooves along the seafloor are punctuated by long rows of spurs, or growths of limestone skeletal substrate that rise up like rugged city skylines. Patch reefs are the other reef structure most often encountered, and might best be described as a coral oasis rising from a barren Atlantic seafloor.

The environment that the hard and soft corals create is akin to an ornate condominium complex teeming with a melting pot of neighbors. Angelfish scales shimmer with emeralds and yellows. Wrasses dart by, their heads the color of billiards chalk. A host of funky crustaceans, including arrow crabs and candy-cane-striped banded shrimp, patrol the corals and sponges like elegant cleaning technicians. Hawksbill and loggerhead turtles, spotted eagle rays, and nurse sharks favor coral reefs, as does the ubiquitous symbol of the Florida Keys, the queen conch.

What might not be so widely known is that all of the best snorkeling is not necessarily found out at the reefs. There are excellent snorkeling opportunities much closer to shore. In some cases, there are corals growing an actual coconut's throw from the beach, albeit a strong throw.

These near-shore snorkeling environments are called hard-bottom coral communities, and while they rarely host the biodiversity found at offshore reefs, they can prove surprising. When snorkeling near shore, it is important to keep your eyes open; from seahorses to manatees, there is no telling when a particular species might reveal itself. Two of the best near-shore snorkeling experiences can be found off the beaches of Bahia Honda and Garden Key down in the Dry Tortugas.

The good news for snorkelers is that it is by no means difficult to find passage out to a given reef. The Florida Keys are absolutely littered with captains and charter boats ferrying snorkelers on a daily basis, generally twice a day, weather permitting.

The ready accessibility of the Florida Reef makes it a very special place, perhaps to its detriment. It is not every barrier reef system that one is able to drive a car down a civilized road lined with motels, bars, souvenir shops, and restaurants, pull off into the parking lot of a snorkeling charter outfit, pay, board, and be in the water looking down at corals in, sometimes, a matter of minutes.

Today, GPS (Global Positioning System) units create straight navigational lines to and around the reef system. Such GPS units take the guesswork out of navigating and allow for precise sites along the expanse of the Florida Reef to be easily accessed. The barrier reef system provides hundreds of excellent snorkeling sites. *Snorkeling the Florida Keys* delves into over 40 of them, including reefs, wrecks, and beaches.

Responsible Snorkeling

Corals are not plants.

Look, do not touch.

When standing up in flippers, be a careful Godzilla.

Be conscientious when kicking.

Respect harvesting rules and no-take zones.

Boaters should anchor in a sandy area away from the reef and swim to the coral.

Cover up with a shirt or sunscreen.

1

Biscayne National Park

The Florida Reef begins to rise from the Atlantic seafloor about 100 miles north of Miami. Where it really starts to blossom, however, is Biscayne National Park. The waters encompassing the park represent the first real chance for snorkelers to explore the full-blown glory that is the Florida Reef.

First established as the smaller Biscayne National Monument in 1968, the park was broadened by President Carter in 1980. Today the park encompasses 181,500 acres of sparkling turquoise water, 20 miles of mangrove-encrusted shoreline, and over 40 scattered keys, including Soldier, Rubicon, Elliot, Old Rhodes, Sands, and Swan Keys.

The park's waters offer a variety of snorkeling opportunities, including seagrass shallows close to shore, the reefs a little further out, and a host of shipwrecks. For instance, just north of Caesar Creek, Sandwich Cove (GPS: 25 25.000N/80 13.000W) is an excellent place to float in the shallows and investigate a hard-bottom coral community.

Snorkelers exploring elkhorn coral in Biscayne National Park. Courtesy of John Brooks, National Park Service.

The cove is sparsely festooned with soft corals and low-profile stony corals, as well as beds of emerald seagrass where conch and starfish are sometimes spotted. The important thing to remember about these near-shore communities is that the fish more closely associated with offshore reefs, such as angelfish and butterflyfish, are often spotted closer in. Usually, however, snorkelers will see a collection of snappers and grunts, parrotfish, and the occasional silvery barracuda.

Should the weather be rough, the wind high, and the surface of the water foamed with a meringue better suited to key lime pie, this protected area can prove an excellent alternative to the reefs and wrecks offshore.

As for suitable snorkeling reefs, a number can be found in the park, including Elkhorn, Triumph, Pacific, Long, Emerald, and Shark reefs. One of the best snorkeling reefs the park has to offer is Ball Buoy Reef (GPS: 25 19.097N/80 11.059W).

This shallow patch reef grows in 8 to 10 feet of water. Yellowtail snapper, Bermuda chubs, and vertically striped black-and-yellow fish called sergeant majors school near the surface, while the more colorful damselfish, gobies, and other assorted tropical fish keep closer to the corals.

Biscayne National Park is also home to one of the great snorkeling wrecks Florida has to offer, the *Mandalay* (GPS: 25 26.530N /80 07.301W). The 122-foot, two-masted steel schooner struck Long Reef on New Year's Day in 1966, and the coral-and-sponge-encrusted skeleton of the ship now rests in 10 to 15 feet of water.

The year before it sank, the schooner was purchased by Windjammer Cruises, Incorporated and refitted with mahogany, brass, ivory, and teak. The ship became part of Windjammer's Barefoot Charter fleet.

The luxury sailing ship was returning from a 10-day trip to the Bahamas with 23 vacationers and 12 crew members on board when it encountered high winds and 10-foot waves. It did not help that the captain had miscalculated his position and was 20 miles off course.

After the ship ran afoul of the corals, the Coast Guard rescued the passengers and crew, all of whom were forced to leave their belongings behind. By the time salvage tugs arrived on the scene to try and dislodge the vessel, it had been virtually picked clean by passing boaters. Today, the ship's frame is a living skeleton teeming with reef fish, hard and soft corals, and colorful crustaceans.

In summer months, park rangers offer guided snorkeling adventures along the Maritime Heritage Trail, a shipwreck trail of five vessels that includes the wreck of the *Mandalay*. The snorkeling trail also includes the *Alicia* (1905), the *Arratoon Apcar* (1878), *Erl King* (1891), and the *Lugano* (1913), the largest ship to that point to have succumbed to the Florida Reef.

Biscayne National Park is also home to one of the more colorful tales alleging piratical operations in the waters surrounding the Florida Keys. For the record, no empirical evidence has ever been provided to authenticate stories of pirates basing their operations in the Florida Keys.

This is not to say that piratical events have not occurred here. They have. Pirates were no strangers to the Reef or the Keys and regularly sailed the area. What historians question is whether or not any of them used the islands as a base of operations.

Suffice it to say that there are not legions of pirate tales associated with the Florida Reef, but there are some. Rear Admiral Caspar F. Goodrich studied the evidence of piratical activity in 1818 and published his findings in the *U.S. Navy Proceedings Magazine*, Volume 42.

Among a number of other incidences involving pirates, Goodrich noted one particular event when he wrote, "To these must be added the ship *Emma Sophia*, from Hamburg to Havana, which was boarded on December 19, by a piratical schooner of 30 tons, 1 gun, 30 men, between Bahama Bank and Sal Key Bank. The ship was sent to a small port formed by the Florida Isles and the Martyr's Reef, and was plundered to the tune of $5,000."

William Savage was the supercargo, or supervisor of cargo, of the *Emma Sophia*. In an excerpt from one of his letters, which was printed in the *Boston Daily Advertiser* "Marine Journal" on February 3, 1819, Savage gave a firsthand account of the events of that horrifying day.

Davis, the spokesman, drew his knife and swore, that every man should die, unless he found the money, and first he would hang the supercargo. He called for a rope, which he had brought on board, fitted with a hangman's noose, sent a man up the mizzen yard and rove it and brought the noose down—and one man held it, and another stood ready to hoist. Now, said Davis, tell me where is the money, where are your diamonds, or I will hang you this minute. In vain I repeated I had nothing more but my watch, which I offered and he refused. Once more, said he, will you tell? I have nothing to tell, said I. On with the rope, said the villain, and hoist away. The fellow with the noose came towards me, and I sprang overboard. They took me up, after some time apparently insensible. They took off all my cloaths [sic], and laid me on my back on deck, naked as I was born, except having a blanket thrown over me. Here I laid five hours without moving hand or foot. Meanwhile they robbed us of every thing of the least value.

For sailors crossing the Florida Straits, most piracy seemed to cease after President Monroe initiated his Antipiracy Act of 1821. Commodore David Porter was then appointed by the secretary of the navy, Smith Thompson, on December 22, 1822, and sworn "to command the vessels-of-war of the United States on the West India station . . . for the suppression of piracy" (Konstam and Kean 198).

In 1823, Porter's antipiracy squadron arrived at Key West. The squadron included 8 shoal-draft schooners, five 20-oared gun barges, and a steam-powered sidewheel ferry boat to tow the barges (the first steam vessel to see active naval service). At his command were 1,100 soldiers.

Among his vessels was a specialized force of five swift, shallow-draft ships capable of agile maneuvers in shallow waters. The fleet consisted of the *Mosquito*, *Sandfly*, *Gnat*, *Midge*, and *Gallinipper*. A gallinipper is a large mosquito or biting fly. The squadron became known as the Mosquito Fleet.

A drawing by George Harding of wreckers at work on the wrecked ship *Alicia*, from "Wreckers of the Florida Keys" published in *Harper's New Monthly Magazine* (June–November, 1911). Courtesy of Jerry Wilkinson Collection.

The squadron chased the pirates down, ship by ship, and cleared most of them from the Florida Straits and West Indies by 1825. With the pirates gone, the coast was clear for Florida wreckers to freely patrol the reef.

Wreckers have long been considered little better than pirates, though history disproves this. Pirates killed who they wanted and took what they could. Wreckers were legally accountable for their actions. They were brave, dedicated men who largely adhered to a strict credo of saving the crew, cargo, and ship. It was dangerous work, and wreckers braved gale-force conditions to reach a ship in peril. Wreckers were often the first responders, making them, in a manner of speaking, a predecessor to the Coast Guard.

Wreckers were awarded a percentage of the salvaged goods from an operation—generally about 25 percent of what the ship and its cargo were worth. However, as the reef began to be dotted with markers and lighthouses, and as ships switched from sail to steam, shipwrecks declined.

The golden age of wrecking proved to be the 1850s and 1860s. By the end of the century, wrecking was in its twilight years. In fact, the last big shipwreck of the Wrecking Era took place on April 25, 1905, when the *Alicia* struck Biscayne National Park's Ajax Reef.

It was hurricane season when the 334-foot Spanish steamer—bound for Havana and laden with silks, linens, shoes, grand pianos, wine, and rum—was driven onto the reef by tropical-storm-force winds and waves. Just about every wrecker still in the business, from Key West to Nassau to Miami, showed up to the party.

The first licensed wrecking captain to arrive was Key Wester "Hog" Johnson, and as such he became wreck master. The wreck master determined how the salvage operation would be handled, as well as how many crews would be needed and which captains were enlisted to work the job at hand.

Hog Johnson needed more than 50 wrecking outfits to salvage the steamer. It did not take long for problems between the competing factions of Key West and Bahamian wreckers to arise. Nor did it help that both sides reportedly got into the rum. Captain Johnson allegedly settled all disputes by painting a red line down the middle of the ship and declaring that the Bahamians would work one side of the *Alicia* while the Key Westers worked the other. Because Johnson was the wreck master, his word was law.

The *Alicia* proved to be the last big wrecking payday of the Wrecking Era. Ultimately, like the pirates before them, wreckers were forced out of one line of work and into another. Some became fishermen, some farmers, and others smugglers. In 1921, the Wrecking License Bureau closed its doors.

At a Glance

Name: Biscayne National Park
Location: 9700 SW 328th St., Homestead
Phone: 305-230-1120
Park Web site: www.nps.gov/bisc
Snorkel charter Web site: www.biscayneunderwater.com
How to get there: Chartered snorkeling adventures can be arranged through the park's concession, Biscayne National Underwater Park, Inc. The charter operation offers both reef exploration trips as well as near-shore adventures in the bays and mangrove ecosystems of the park's islands.

SNORKELING SITES

Reefs

Anniversary Reef GPS: 25 23.295N/80 09.864W; Depth: 8–12 feet
Bache Shoal   GPS: 25 29.150N/80 09.939W; Depth: 5–15 feet
Ball Buoy Reef GPS: 25 19.097N/80 11.059W; Depth: 8–10 feet

Elkhorn Reef GPS: 25 21.777N/80 09.952W; Depth: 6–12 feet
Emerald Reef GPS: 25 40.450N/80 05.920W; Depth: 15–26 feet
Long Reef GPS: 25 26.630/80 07.603W; Depth: 10–60 feet
Pacific Reef GPS: 25 22.197N/80 08.349W; Depth: 18–22 feet
Shark Reef GPS: 25 20.364N/80 09.944W; Depth: 10–20 feet
Triumph Reef GPS: 25 28.599N/80 06.678W; Depth: 15–20 feet

Shipwrecks

Alicia GPS: 25 24.734N/80 07.642W; Depth: 13–20 feet
Arratoon Apcar GPS: 25 35.506N/80 05.765W; Depth: 25 feet
Erl King GPS: 25 25.479N/80 07.462W; Depth: 20 feet
Lugano GPS: 25 26.681N/80 07.153W; Depth: 20–25 feet
Mandalay GPS: 25 26.530N/80 07.301W; Depth: 10–15 feet

Fun Facts

The 1775 Bernard Romans Chart gives the name Caesar's Rock to the small mangrove islet rising from the pass between Elliot and Old Rhodes Keys. F. H. Gerdes, a nineteenth-century cartographer with the United States Coast and Geodetic Survey, noted in his writings: "Black Caesar's Key is an island, small, between Old Rhodes Key and Elliot's Key (Old Rhodes being nearest to N. of Key Largo): the opening on both sides is called Black Caesar's Creek" (Gerdes 42).

Black Caesar was allegedly an African chieftain captured by slave traders and slated to be auctioned in the Americas. During the Atlantic crossing, the slave ship was swept against the reef by a hurricane.

Two men reportedly survived the wreck, the African chieftain and the only crew member aboard the ship he had been willing to accept food or drink from. They escaped in a longboat, managed to find the safety of dry land, and turned to pirating.

"Captain Teach commonly called Black Beard," reads the caption beneath this Thomas Nichols drawing (circa 1736). Courtesy of Jerry Wilkinson Collection.

Black Caesar, as he came to be known, initially employed the following strategy: upon spying a ship sailing along the reef line, he and his mate would row their longboat out to the reef and make as if adrift. Once "rescued" and brought on board, they would draw arms, demand the ship's treasures, accept those sailors willing to join their crew, and kill the rest.

As Black Caesar's operation grew in both manpower and ships, new strategies had to be developed. One of the problems for pirates operating sailing ships amidst these keys was that there was nowhere to hide a mast. Black Caesar was said to have solved the problem by driving an iron ring into the rocky outcropping of a small island in the middle of the channel separating Elliot and Old Rhodes Key—Black Caesar's Rock. By running a rope through the ring and tying it off to the ship, with sufficient heaving, the ship could be keeled over enough for the masts to dip below the tree line.

Once a passing vessel was sighted, the pirates sent a longboat out to the reef like a fisherman casting a baited hook. If the passing ship slowed to lend aid, Black Caesar ordered the lines restraining the warship cut. Released, the ship would spring to life from behind Elliot Key like a magic trick. Setting the sails, the pirates would charge out of the small creek to go a-plundering.

While some of the specifics may be myth, Black Caesar was a real pirate reported to have ended his career serving aboard *Queen Anne's Revenge,* a 40-gun ship captained by one of the most feared pirates in the whole of the Caribbean, Edward Teach— better known as Blackbeard. The two pirates were apprehended by forces led by Lieutenant Robert Maynard of the Royal Army in November of 1718 off the coast of North Carolina's Ocracoke Island.

Blackbeard's head was subsequently severed and hung from the bowsprit of a Navy ship, as was the practice. Black Caesar was taken to Virginia, where he stood trial, was found guilty of piracy, and hanged.

The iron ring sticking out of Black Caesar's Rock was real. In 1934, however, a Miami Beach resident named Carl Holm reportedly dislodged it and sent it to the Smithsonian Institution (Griswold 14).

2

Carysfort Reef

~~~~~~

Among its list of favorable attributes, one that makes Carysfort Reef such a desirable snorkeling destination, is its location—south of Biscayne National Park, and at the northernmost reaches of that snorkeling haven, John D. Pennekamp Coral Reef State Park. Because it is in a relative snorkeling charter no-man's-land, it is less frequently visited than some of the other Upper Keys reefs and thus is more pristine.

While technically within the Pennekamp Park boundaries, because of its northern locale, it is uncommon for Key Largo charter outfits to visit the reef. Instead, they tend to concentrate on snorkeling destinations closer to their home port, largely due to time and fuel considerations.

Carysfort Reef is an extensive reef system that stretches for 4 miles in the shallow Atlantic waters approximately 6 miles off the coast of North Key Largo. Because depths range from a mere 5 to 25 feet, the reef is sublimely suited to snorkeling.

It is also one of the oldest, most mature reefs in the chain, the result of thousands of years of tedious work by reef-building coral polyps. In fact, once upon a time, vast forests of elkhorn and stag-horn corals rose from the substrate like great branching crowns. Because of those thorny crowns, Carysfort Reef has, historically speaking, been the most dangerous tract of coral to ships attempting to make the passage through the Florida Straits.

The terrible Florida reef, with its bewildering maze of shoals, tortuous channels, fierce currents and coral heads lifted almost to the surface, is an ever present menace to the mariners of the waters. Since the date of its discovery it has probably been the cause of more disasters than any other region of similar extent in the world. (Munroe 89)

There was a time when the southernmost reaches of the Bermuda Triangle were blamed for the inordinately high number of shipwrecks here. The real explanation was simpler than devilish forces—it was always coral, lots and lots of coral. Coral grows so near the surface here that when the Atlantic washes over some of the shallower reef heads, a light meringue is left behind.

It only seems natural then that this particular reef is home to the oldest recorded shipwreck in North America, that of the HMS *Winchester*. The 60-gun British warship was built in Bursledon, England, in 1693, and at just over 146 feet long and 38 feet wide, the square-rigged vessel maintained a crew of 285 sailors and soldiers.

Edward Bibb was captain of the ship when it left England with orders to sail to the West Indies. One aspect of the *Winchester's* mission was to disrupt French business in the southern latitudes, as the two countries were at war. To that end, while in the Caribbean, the *Winchester*, along with the support of another 60-gun warship, the *Dunkirk*, made a successful raid against the French colony called St. Dominique (now known as Haiti) in January of 1695.

After the attack, both the *Winchester* and the *Dunkirk*, along with a captured French brigantine, sailed to the temporary home port of Kingston. Part of Jamaica's infamous Port Royal had fallen into the Caribbean after a devastating earthquake just two years prior, in 1693.

In Kingston, however, all was not well aboard the *Winchester*. Men were dying as quickly as one a day. Some accounts attribute these deaths to scurvy, others yellow fever. Scurvy seems to make less sense, as there would have been loads of citrus available while in this port where, it is reported, 140 men eventually succumbed to disease. Among the dead was Captain Bibb who, before his death, had relegated his duties to John Soule.

In September, while the death toll aboard the *Winchester* continued to rise, Captain Soule sailed it out of Kingston Harbor close behind the *Dunkirk* and the captured French brigantine. But he too fell ill and, no longer able to perform his duties as captain, relegated his command to the next in line, Master Andrew Mallard.

Aboard ship only 60 men were still alive, and of those survivors, only 10 were deemed healthy enough to work. As if things were not going poorly enough, just after midnight on September 24, 1695, the *Winchester* struck Carysfort Reef hard and fast. It would never dislodge.

Seeing the *Winchester* in peril, the captain of the *Dunkirk* ordered the French brigantine to approach the wreck and rescue the surviving crew. No doubt he was unwilling to expose the men aboard his ship to the malady plaguing the wrecked ship.

Captain Soule sustained injuries in the wreck, but survived to be taken aboard the French brig, where he would later die. As for the ship, it succumbed to the reef, spilling its cannons to the ocean floor where, more than 200 years later, they would be discovered by two Miami fishermen, Sam Lynch and Jacob Munroe.

The *Winchester* was not, however, the ship to leave the most indelible mark on the reef. That dubious honor goes to the HMS *Carysfort*, a 118-foot British frigate armed with twenty-four 9-pound cannons, four 3-pound cannons, and a number of guns on swivels. It hit the reef on October 23, 1770. The good news about the *Carysfort* is that no one lost their lives, the ship was ultimately refloated, and it sailed away.

The Carysfort Reef corals continued to wreak havoc on those merchant vessels using the Florida Straits to traffic goods between South America, New Orleans, New York, and Europe. It must have proved anything but surprising when government officials acknowledged the need to mark the reef relatively early on.

The first attempt to mark the reef occurred in 1824 when Congress allocated $20,000 to produce a lightship to be anchored out at the reef. The ship was built with two masts, each equipped with a lantern-based light source that, when lit, would theoretically be visible for a distance of 12 miles. The ship was also rigged with bells that would clank, broadcasting the sound over the ocean's surface with every swell.

The end result was the *Caesar*, a 220-ton two-lantern schooner built in New York by Henry Eckford. The ship was finished and left New York, bound for the Florida Reef, the following year. It was not a smooth trip: the *Caesar* encountered squally weather, high winds, and nasty seas, and was eventually blown ashore near Key Biscayne. The transport crew abandoned the ship, and it was later salvaged by wreckers who brought it to Key West for repairs. Back in port, John Whalton, its new captain, was waiting.

After the *Caesar* was repaired, restocked, and re-crewed, Captain Whalton set sail for Turtle Harbor, a safe anchorage near Carysfort Reef. While the lightship did its best to light the reef, the system had flaws, especially during inclement weather. Suffice it to say that the light was not always visible, or became so too late.

While the *Caesar* was a good first step, a more permanent marker was being planned, as ships were still running aground on the reef. One of the more unsavory wrecks was that of the *Guerrero*. The ship hit the reef not so much because it was improperly lit, but because of the captain's desperation. He was a slaver taking his chances for a big paycheck, and the result was horrific.

The Spanish *Guerrero* held 561 African slaves when it attempted to outrun the British warship HMS *Nimble*. The *Guerrero* slammed into Carysfort on December 19, 1827, with sufficient force to snap its twin masts. Forty Africans drowned in the hold. The rest were "rescued." The *Nimble* also ran aground that night, but would be refloated and sail away relatively unscathed.

Captain John Whalton heard the exchange of cannon fire between the two vessels while stationed aboard the *Caesar* at Turtle Harbor. John Whalton is quoted as saying, "I saw the flash and heard the report of seven or eight guns," according to sources used in an article by Willie Drye, "Explorers Search for Slave Shipwreck Off Florida," published in *National Geographic News* on July 30, 2004.

In only a handful of years the *Caesar*, too, would be lost, though not to the reef per se. The lightship succumbed to the environment and did so epically. A paltry six years into service, the vessel was sailed to Key West for inspection.

It did not fare well. After his survey of the ship, the collector of customs remarked of the *Caesar*'s timbers, "an entire mass of dry rot and fungus. I must say that there never was a grosser imposition practiced than by the contractor in this instance" (Viele, *Florida Keys, vol. 1,* 38).

The *Caesar* was condemned. Congress again allotted $20,000 for the construction of another lightship to mark the reef. This next ship, the *Florida*, was built by the same contractor in New York, though this time with rot-resistant live oak timber. Upon its

At one time, Carysfort Light, constructed in 1852, was considered haunted. Courtesy of Jerry Wilkinson Collection.

delivery, Captain Whalton promptly took command of the *Florida* and resumed his post at Turtle Harbor.

Early on in his tenure Captain Whalton realized that supply ships could prove unreliable. To combat this inconvenience, he maintained a garden of melons and tomatoes on a clearing of land on North Key Largo. On June 26, 1837, Captain Whalton and four of his crew lowered a boat from the *Florida*, manned the oars, and rowed ashore to tend the garden.

When they stepped onto land, they were greeted by the gunfire of Seminole Indian warriors. Whalton and one of his crew were shot, killed, and scalped. Three crew members escaped back to the *Florida*. These murders helped incite the Second Seminole War.

Out on the water, Carysfort was still proving to be a terribly dangerous reef. "Partial returns of the number of wrecks from 1833 to 1841, inclusive, make a list of 324 vessels, 63 of which went on to the Carysfort Reef, or nearly 20 per cent" (Enoch and Rhoads 108).

One of the reasons for this bloated number, however, may be that during those early years of sailing (and of record-keeping), Carysfort Reef was used as a generic term for all North Key Largo wrecks. It was not, however, the only reason. Another reason ships were still wrecking on the reef might best be summed up in a letter dated July 1851, written by Lieutenant David D. Porter, U.S. Navy, commander of the U.S. mail-steamer *Georgia*. "On the reef near Cape Large," he wrote, "the floating lightship, showing two lights, intended to be seen twelve miles, but they are scarcely discernible from the outer ledge of Carysfort Reef, which is from four to five miles distant. On to [*sic*] occasions I have passed it at night, when the lights were either very dim or not lighted" (U.S. Light-House Board 741).

By the time the letter had been written, however, Congress had already allocated funds for the construction of a permanent light to mark the reef. Captain Howard Stansbury of the U.S. Army

Corps of Topographical Engineers took command of the project in 1848.

Stansbury managed to oversee the formation of the base for a 112-foot lighthouse before retiring from the project. He was replaced by Major Thomas B. Linnard, who died a short time later. Lieutenant George Meade finished the Carysfort job in 1852. Carysfort would not be the last lighthouse Meade helped construct along the Florida Reef.

Considering the history of Carysfort Reef, it should come as no surprise that the lighthouse would ultimately be called haunted, at least for a time. Lighthouse keepers were said to place an open Bible inside the structure to thwart the ghost's devilish intrusions.

Charles M. Brookfield, a local fisherman, treasure hunter, and writer, happened to spend the night at the structure in 1927. During his stay, Brookfield was startled awake by a shriek reverberating through the lighthouse. When the ghoulish sound recurred, Brookfield grabbed his flashlight and ran up the spiral staircase to the light, where he found Harry Baldwin working.

"Harry," he asked, "have you ever heard any funny noises down below?"

"Oh sure," Harry said, "but we don't pay attention to 'em any more. It's only Captain Johnson, and he just comes around to see if all's well. He died out here on the light, you know. Must have been a great sinner, he moans so. Sometimes he rattles his chains." (Brookfield 69)

Unconvinced of the nature of the noise, Brookfield postulated that the screech was the result of metal expanding and contracting due to temperature fluctuations. It certainly explained why the "ghost" only appeared in the hot summer months.

Just a decade later, in 1939, the light keepers were replaced by a more official crew. The Presidential Reorganization Act incorporated all lights and lighthouses in U.S. waters into the U.S. Coast Guard.

"Coastie" Frank Taylor was 21 when he was assigned to Carysfort Light in 1957. In an interview with Marjorie Doughty, Taylor was quoted as saying, "It was almost like I was being taken to Alcatraz" (Doughty, "Life on the Light").

While life aboard the light could be tedious, it was not all work and no play. In the article, Taylor recalled learning how to snorkel.

Allen Riddle of Atlantic City taught me. He was really down to earth. He knew everything about snorkeling. We got to be pretty tight and he showed me how to go down at night with a shark hook. That was great because there was really nothing to do. We did a little scraping and painting, had a small black and white television with bad reception and there were a few books. So, I learned to catch fish with a spear gun and we would look at the fisherman and call them "worm drowners."

The lighthouse became fully automated in 1960, and the Coast Guard servicemen left their posts for other duties. Surprisingly, with all the advances in technology, ships have still managed to find the reef on occasion. The last major wreck at Carysfort was that of the *Maitland*.

Despite the fact that the massive light was in operation at the time, the captain of the 155-foot, 244-ton vessel managed to lodge his ship atop the shallow reef on October 24, 1989. He then made the worst possible decision—he put the ship into reverse and tried to power off the corals.

His actions caused a substantial swath of reef to be crushed and destroyed. When the crater-sized holes the wreck left behind threatened to undermine the stability of the reef, Harold Hudson, affectionately referred to in the Keys as the Reef Doctor, organized a team to repair and reconstruct the reef using concrete slabs.

Barracuda are seen at almost every snorkeling site. They look menacing but are more curious than dangerous. Courtesy of Jeff Anderson, Florida Keys National Marine Sanctuary.

Although Carysfort Reef has taken a beating, it still makes for an amazing snorkel. The reef's proximity to the Gulf Stream means visibility remains generally excellent. Carysfort has remained one of the healthier reefs in the chain due, at least in part, to the fact that it is not regularly visited by the Key Largo charter trade. The reef remains festooned with a broad expanse of hard and soft corals, as well as a resurging sponge population.

For those snorkelers looking to get up close and personal with the smaller creatures of the reef—the worms, snails, and other crustaceans making their living atop the corals—explore the shallows surrounding the base of the light. It is an excellent opportunity to observe Christmas tree fan worms that sprout up like, well, tiny colorful Christmas trees. Get too close, however, and the worms will retract back into their homes.

In addition to the ample supply of bicolored damselfish, blue-headed wrasses, butterflyfish, and angelfish, the reef is home to large schools of the usual collection of snappers, grunts, and parrotfish. Spotted eagle rays and turtles are also common visitors.

However, be careful when attempting to navigate the shallower coral beds. All it takes is one swell of the ocean to push a snorkeler over the sharp corals; the result can prove painful and even a little bloody.

At a Glance

Name: Carysfort Reef
How to get there: Carysfort Reef proves one of the trickier sites to visit for those snorkelers without the benefit of their own boat. The spur-and-groove reef is ideal for snorkelers, with depths ranging from 5 to 25 feet, but most of the operations headed in this direction cater to the scuba crowd. For those interested in seeking a charter on any particular day, the best bet is to contact North Key Largo charter outfits and inquire if a snorkeling trip to Carysfort is on their agenda.

SNORKELING SITES

Reefs

Carysfort Reef   GPS: 25 13.314N/80 12.690W; Depth: 5–25 feet

Shipwrecks

Winchester   GPS: 25 12.178N/80 13.516W; Depth: 15–30 feet

Fun Facts

The two fishermen who originally discovered the shipwreck of the *Winchester* told Elliot Key resident Charles M. Brookfield of the site. Brookfield and a group of local treasure hunters dove on the site in December of 1938 and used markings carved on the cannons to identify the wreck as that of the *Winchester*.

Technically, the ship ran afoul of what is referred to as South Carysfort Reef, as this is, remember, a four-mile-long stretch of coral reef. Not much remains of the ship, but its ballast stones can be found with careful inspection. The scant remains can be found in 15 to 30 feet of water.

3

John D. Pennekamp
Coral Reef State Park

More than a million people visit the world's first underwater park every year, and a great many of them have snorkeling on their minds. With myriad coral reefs and shipwrecks to explore, Pennekamp is the quintessential destination for anyone looking to get their snorkel on. In the Florida Keys, in fact, Pennekamp is practically synonymous with snorkeling.

John D. Pennekamp Coral Reef State Park is the only park in the archipelago that really caters to snorkelers, offering multiple trips from their expansive docks daily, weather permitting. Masks, snorkels, and sunscreen are all available at the park's concession. In fact, everything necessary to dive in and explore the Florida Reef can be had here, and for that very reason, the park is a beacon.

This is both a good and a bad thing. While it is the perfect family destination, the park can also become quite crowded. If the park has a downside, it is its wild popularity, especially on weekends. On holiday weekends, the park sometimes closes because crowds have swelled the acreage to capacity.

Discussing the Coral Reef Park without first mentioning the man responsible for helping to bring it to life, however, would be tantamount to having a cool slice of key lime pie without first sampling some of the local favorites: the spiny lobster, stone crab, or hogfish.

The park's namesake, John D. Pennekamp, was born in Ohio on January 1, 1897. He was working as a copy boy for the *Cincinnati Post* by 14. At 28 he packed his bags and left Ohio to cover one of the big news stories of the day, the Miami land bust. Mr. Pennekamp relocated to the eastern edge of Florida's swampland.

Fortunately he was not put off by South Florida's oppressive humidity, hurricanes, or mosquitoes. Not everyone who visits this sultry corner of America can take the heat. But Mr. Pennekamp, or "Penny" to his friends, fell in love with Florida's subtropical charms and never left.

John Pennekamp was a passionate writer who spent more than 50 years working for the *Miami Herald* in various capacities, including editor, daily columnist, and managing editor. Whether or not he would refer to himself as such, he was a bona fide conservationist who used his keen eye and crafty pen like a watchdog. According to then-Florida-governor LeRoy Collins, "His pen has struck down the despoiler and exalted those who would conserve" (Brookfield 66).

The coral reef was not, however, the first environment Pennekamp championed. He had more than a passing hand in the transformation of the public's perception of the Everglades: from a maligned swampland of saw grass and alligators into a biological gem worth protecting. Everglades National Park was dedicated by President Truman on December 6, 1947. The swamps and alligators had achieved lawful protection.

The elephant trumpeting in the room for Mr. Pennekamp, however, was indeed the Florida Reef. The editor was outraged at the systematic rape, pillage, and dynamiting of the coral reef in order to satisfy the souvenir trade. "The situation has become desperate," said Pennekamp. "The souvenir purveyors are out there with barges taking it apart."

Meanwhile, at a meeting held on Pine Island, 52 scientists gathered to plead for the conservation of the Florida Reef. Dr. Gilbert Voss of the University of Miami's Institute of Marine Science predicted that if current practices continued unabated, the coral reef system would become barren. When asked what would destroy the coral reef, Dr. Voss replied, "Man" (Brookfield 65).

So a plan was devised to create a sanctuary that would help protect at least a small segment of the coral reef system, one that was largely water-based. In 1959, the Coral Reef Reserve was proposed. In order to make the park a reality, Governor LeRoy Collins had to release the state's control of the ocean bottom from the shoreline to the three-mile limit. The federal government, too, needed to relinquish its water rights from the state's three-mile jurisdiction to the three-hundred-foot depth line.

As the state and federal legalities were being figured out, the reef was still being dismantled. Queen conch shells and corals were being ripped and scoured from the reefs, loaded into barges, and shipped off on a daily basis. Tropical fish were also being captured to satisfy a burgeoning aquarium trade.

The good news was that the Coral Reef Reserve set a record for the shortest period from proposal to opening day. "Seldom has an idea gained such momentum with so little resistance," remarked Dr. Voss (Griswold 143).

The world's first underwater park was officially dedicated at Tavernier's Harry Harris Park on December 10, 1960. During the course of the ceremony, Governor LeRoy Collins took the liberty of changing the name from simply the Coral Reef Park to the John D. Pennekamp Coral Reef State Park in honor of the man who had shown himself a Palladium of South Florida's natural resources.

The ceremony was held in Tavernier because, while the Coral Reef Park had secured all the necessary water rights, they had no land component. It was fortunate that Penny was on the job, because he was aware that the Rand Trust, in partnership with Radford Crane, had 74 acres of prime Key Largo real estate for sale.

Unfortunately, there was already an offer of $141,000 for the land on the table. This fact did not stop Mr. Pennekamp from introducing himself to Mr. Crane. He met with the man, unrolled the maps to the proposed park, and made his pitch for the land. An August 4, 1966, article from the *Miami Herald* recorded the conversation.

> Pennekamp, speaking to Mr. Crane, asked, "if he would delay action on the offer until I could find out whether the state would buy it."
>
> "When would that be?"
>
> "I am sure the Park Service wants the land, but we will probably have to wait until the Legislature meets again, then ask for the appropriation."
>
> "Will they make the appropriation?"
>
> "Honestly, I do not know. I don't believe any similar action has ever been taken before, and there is probably only an even chance."
>
> Crane was said to have studied the maps for a few minutes before he looked back up at Pennekamp.
>
> "Forget it. I'll give it to you. I'll have to get the consent of my family, but they usually go along with me."

Work on the land base of the Coral Reef Park began in January 1962, and by August the park's master plan had been brought to fruition. Ellison Hardee was named the park's first superintendent.

Mr. Pennekamp later ran into Crane at a luncheon and reintroduced himself. Pennekamp said, "When you have time, I would

Pictured from left to right are Joe Fredricks, John Pennekamp, Park Superintendent Ellison Hardee, and Johnny Johnson. Courtesy of Jerry Wilkinson
Collection.

like to take you down to see the work that is being done to the
Coral Reef Park."

"I've seen it," Crane replied, "and we want to give some more.
I'll have my attorney call you tomorrow."

The additional acreage donated by Crane increased the park's
land base to three miles of oceanfront property. The appraised
value of the property was $2.35 million, making it the largest gift
ever made in the United States to a state park. It was not, however,
the last gift the Coral Reef Park would receive.

For starters, when the acquired lands were insufficient to connect the park to the Overseas Highway, Herbert and Donna Shaw donated 50 crucial feet of land to provide a driveway. Then, when the park officially opened to the public in 1963, the gifts kept coming.

Egidi Cressi, an Italian skin diving enthusiast, donated a nine-foot bronze statue, today called the Christ of the Deep, to the Underwater Society of America. That statue, the third bronze casting of the original sculpture created by Guido Galletti, was passed on to the state park system, where it eventually found its way to the Coral Reef Reserve.

Today the statue, which rests comfortably beneath the turquoise waters at Key Largo Dry Rocks (GPS: 25 07.450N/80 18.312W), is the single most photographed image on the Florida Reef. To help ensure the statue's stability, it was reinforced by a concrete base. The nearly 20,000-pound combination of statue and base were soon tested by Betsy, a Category 3 hurricane that ruffled Key Largo on September 8, 1965. The statue did not budge, and the Christ of the Deep was later dedicated by John Pennekamp on June 29, 1966.

Today the park encompasses an area of approximately 70 nautical square miles filled with mangroves, seagrass, and coral reefs that starts near Carysfort Reef to the north and stretches 21 miles south to Molasses Reef. However, one thing should be made clear. It is not possible to drive into Pennekamp Park, park the car, strap on a mask and fins, and snorkel over the corals.

The coral reefs are several miles offshore and require a boat to reach them. Do not be confused by those people snorkeling off the small beach across the parking lot from the visitor's center. While the beach is perfect for lounging, this is not the snorkeling experience that has made the park world famous.

The shallows off the beach are filled with fields of seagrass, not corals, and while the odd snapper, barracuda, or southern stingray

Ellison Hardee looking back at the Statue of the Deep, circa 1965, before it was transported to Key Largo Dry Rocks. Courtesy of Jerry Wilkinson Collection.

might patrol the beds from time to time in search of a crab or some other succulent tidbit, these waters do not represent the riches Pennekamp has to offer.

There is also a replica cannon in the shallows that can attract small grouper and colorful parrotfish.

It is an excellent locale in which to splash around or, better yet, for first-time snorkelers to acclimate to their snorkeling gear.

The real snorkeling treat is waiting out at the reefs, and rest assured that park concessionaires are doing their best to make visiting them as easy as possible. Masks, fins, and snorkels can be rented from the Snorkel Shed near the marina. Charter boats leave the Pennekamp docks two or three times a day, depending on the time of year.

For those snorkelers traveling in mixed company, it is important to keep in mind that the snorkeling charter boats operating out of Pennekamp do not accommodate scuba divers, though they do offer a separate scuba charter twice daily. And for anyone who wants to see the coral reef, but has no intention of dipping a single toe into the water, Pennekamp's glass-bottomed boat, *Discovery*, also departs from the dock daily. Finally, the park also rents boats for those looking to explore the reefs on their own.

Snorkelers have a shipload of options inside the park. Two of the more prominent reefs are Carysfort Reef (GPS: 25 13.3140N/80 12.690W), which is located at the northern reaches of the park, and Molasses Reef (GPS: 25 00.579N/80 22.471W) at the other end.

Grecian Rocks (GPS: 25 06.711N/80 18.312W) is also a Pennekamp favorite. The rocky structures are perfect for snorkeling and range from the surface to about 35 feet. It is important to remember, especially when snorkeling over these particularly shallow areas, to be hyperaware of what is in the immediate area. A single swipe from an errant flipper can undo decades of hard coral labor, and damaging corals is not what John D. Pennekamp had in mind when he fought for the creation of this park.

At a Glance

Name: John D. Pennekamp Coral Reef State Park
Web site: www.floridastateparks.org/pennekamp/

Location: MM 102.5, Key Largo

How to get there: The land portion of the park can be accessed directly from the Overseas Highway near Mile Marker 102.5, Oceanside. The park is the epitome of the full-service snorkeling facility. Everything from equipment rental to charter boats is provided, including glass bottom boat excursions. All charters depart from the Pennekamp docks at a minimum of twice daily. It should be noted that it is unnecessary to drive into the park to access a snorkeling charter scheduled to explore the reefs inside park boundaries. The truth is that most, if not all, snorkeling charters operating in the area service the underwater boundaries of Pennekamp.

SNORKELING SITES

Reefs

Carysfort Reef   GPS: 25 13.314N/80 12.690W; Depth: 0–80 feet
Elbow Reef   GPS: 25 08.820N/80 15.190W; Depth: 15–85 feet
French Reef   GPS: 25 02.057N/80 20.893W; Depth: 12–40 feet
Grecian Rocks   GPS: 25 06.711N/80 18.312W; Depth: 5–25 feet
Horseshoe Reef   GPS: 25 08.362N/80 17.641W; Depth: 8–22 feet
Key Largo Dry Rocks (Christ of the Deep)   GPS: 25 06.91N/80 18.20W; Depth: 0–30 feet
North Dry Rocks   GPS: 25 07.840N/80 17.660W; Depth: 5–25 feet
North North Dry Rocks   GPS: 25 08.274N/80 17.336W; Depth: 5–25 feet
Molasses Reef   GPS: 25 00.579N/80 22.471W; Depth: 10–40 feet
Turtle Reef/Rocks   GPS: 25 16.927N/80 12.425W; Depth: 0–30 feet

Shipwrecks

City of Washington   GPS: 25 08.786N/80 15.354W; Depth: 15–25 feet

Fun Facts

An earlier model of the glass-bottomed boat *Discovery* was featured in the 1976 comic book, *Dennis the Menace in Florida*. Hank Ketcham, creator and writer of *Dennis the Menace*, visited Pennekamp and afterward inserted Dennis into a Florida adventure. While Dennis never got to snorkel over the reef, he could see snorkelers and scuba divers exploring the reef through *Discovery*'s glass bottom. The tour guide narrating the adventure over the loudspeaker said, "The next time, explore our country's only coral reef in person!"

"Yeah!" Dennis exclaimed to his parents, "Let's do that!"

Above: Mix of hard and soft corals.

Below: French angelfish.

Above: Flamingo tongue snail.

Right: Coral polyps, close-up.

Above: Juvenile puddingwife wrasse, sea fan in background.

Below: Hawksbill turtle, French angelfish in background.

Above: Rock beauty.

Below: Juvenile beau gregory.

Above: Smooth trunkfish.

Below: Nurse shark with yellowtail snapper in background.

Above: Queen angelfish.

Left: Banded coral shrimp on moray eel.

Above: Remora on Spanish hogfish.

Below: Scrawled filefish.

Left: A cushion star found patrolling the seagrass shallows near Indian Key.

Below: Soft coral bonanza featuring elegant stands of sea fans.

4

City of Washington

~~~~~~

Elbow Reef rises from the Atlantic substrate 5.3 miles southwest of Carysfort Lighthouse. It is a relatively shallow spur-and-groove reef system growing at the eastern edge of the Pennekamp boundary in 10 to 35 feet of water. Once upon a time it was considered a fairly dangerous reef and marked with a 36-foot tower.

It is not just another reef, however, and offers snorkelers something more than tropical fish and coral. The Elbow was once a ship killer, and the remains of its victims are clearly visible beneath the surface. One of the causes of shipwrecks at this particular reef has always been the interesting direction the corals decided to go when they began building thousands of years ago—toward the clear, warm, nutrient-rich waters of the Gulf Stream. The resulting reef formation juts out toward the current like, well, an elbow.

Snorkelers will see a virtual farmer's field of lacy purple sea fans ebbing and flowing with the currents as well as the usual collection of snappers, grunts, and porkfish schooling about. Bullish damselfish and darting wrasses will be found closer to the substrate.

Because the reef is located particularly close to the Gulf Stream, it is acutely affected by current. This is both a blessing and a curse.

On the one hand, visibility is generally excellent because the current washes the reef in clear blue water. On the other hand, when the current is really strong, swimming against it can prove an unpleasant, even exhausting, experience.

What the reef is most famous for, however, are the skeletal remains of a number of wrecked ships that decorate the sandy seafloor. Perhaps none of these drowned vessels is more storied than the *City of Washington*. Of the area wrecks, this particular ship remains one of the most prominent.

City of Washington was one of two ships commissioned by Alexander and Sons at the Chester, Pennsylvania, shipyard. The ship was built for the general transport of mail, cargo, and passengers. At just over 300 feet long, it was a little bit longer than a football field.

It was also a hybrid vessel, designed in those transitional times between sail and full-blown steam. As such, it not only boasted double masts equipped with sails, but twin, high-performance, compound surface-condensing engines built by the Morgan Iron Works manufacturing plant in New York City.

When it launched from Roach's Shipyard, an 1877 edition of the *Chester Daily Times* reported that the ship "could accommodate 100 first class passengers, with 75 staterooms, besides accommodations for officers, crew, and 250 steerage passengers." To picture steerage accommodations, think of Leonardo DiCaprio's belowdecks digs in the movie *Titanic*.

With 1,900 employees, Roach was a serious builder responsible for the manufacturing of over 60 ships between 1872 and 1881. The year after *City of Washington* was launched, Alexander and Sons merged with the competing Ward Line to form the New York and Cuba Mail and Steamship Company. Mr. Roach, a builder for both lines, also became a partner in the new company.

Though it made use of its original engine for over a year, *City of Washington* was returned to Roach's Shipyard between July 20 and October 12, 1889, to be refitted with a 2,750 horsepower, triple-expansion steam engine. By the time it returned to service, the newly powered *City of Washington* was able to make the run between Havana and New York in 73 hours.

Because the *City of Washington* ferried passengers and mail between New York and Cuba, it happened to spend a fair amount of time moored in Havana Harbor. In those days, America had an economic interest in Cuba and had, in fact, invested $50 million in Cuban sugarcane and tobacco commodities.

Cuba was a West Indies stronghold of the Spanish empire. The Cubans had been unsuccessfully fighting for independence for decades. In the 1890s, however, Cuba's fight for independence began to percolate, due in no small part to José Martí. The future national hero had been stirring the political pot with revolutionary talk.

On January 5, 1892, Martí, wanting Cuba free of both American and Spanish control, formed El Partido Revolucionario Cubano. The exiled poet and teacher proceeded to make multiple tours of Cuban outposts in America, where he began energizing and organizing the Cuban community. An impassioned speaker, Martí garnered support for Cuban independence from those nationals who had emigrated to safer, greener pastures.

He started in New York City before traveling to Philadelphia and Tampa. Naturally, he stopped in Key West to rally those countrymen toiling in the cigar factories. It took a few years to raise the funds necessary to support an army, but on February 24, 1895, Martí declared his *Grito de Baire*, his call to arms.

On his final tour of America, Martí stopped for the last time in Key West, where he stood on the second-story balcony of the San Carlos Institute, 516 Duval Street, and enthralled a crowd of 5,000 people gathered in the street below with declarations of Cuban freedom.

After Key West, Martí traveled around the Caribbean to beat

his war drum, making stops in Haiti, Santo Domingo, and Jamaica. Martí's Liberation Army, led by General-in-Chief Máximo Gómez, attacked in the months to follow, and Martí was killed in combat at Dos Rios on May 19, 1895. While the Liberation Army damaged the Spanish invaders, independence was not achieved at this juncture. It would come, later, with a little American intervention. Suffice it to say that by the time June rolled around, the political climate in the Caribbean was nearly at a boil.

President Cleveland proclaimed neutrality in the growing Cuban crisis. He had a change of heart, however, when Spanish general Valeriano Weyler, nicknamed the Butcher, began to strategically center the Cuban population in strictly Spanish strongholds. President Cleveland reversed his stance on the growing Cuban crisis, but was voted out of office.

William McKinley became the twenty-fifth president of the United States. He was inaugurated on March 4, 1897. Not a full year into his presidency, on February 9, 1898, a personal letter written by Spanish foreign minister Enrique Dupuy de Lôme was printed in the *New York Journal*—as well as a number of other newspapers and journals. The letter called McKinley "weak and a bidder of the admiration of the crowd."

The Bronx cheer prompted President McKinley to send a second-class battleship, the USS *Maine*, to Cuba as a show of America's willingness to protect its interests on the island. The warship pulled into Havana Harbor in broad daylight on January 25, 1898, with nearly 400 crewmen on board. In the days that followed, *City of Washington* also pulled into the harbor and moored near the battleship.

While the events that were to follow have never been fully explained, what is clear is that both the *Maine* and the *City of Washington* were in port on the night of February 15—the night when

This photograph of the USS *Maine* was copyrighted by J. S. Johnson in 1896.
Courtesy of Jerry Wilkinson Collection.

everything suddenly went to bloody hell. The forward gunpowder magazine of the USS *Maine* exploded.

Between the initial blast and the ship's subsequent sinking, nearly 300 sailors were lost. Shrapnel damaged the awnings and deckhouses of the nearby *City of Washington*. Its crew, however, managed to pluck over 90 survivors of the *Maine* from the turbulent water. Survivors were shipped to Key West.

At the time, the cause of the blast was never completely determined, and two theories have since been floated. The first is that the explosion was caused by a submarine mine. The second theory suggests that the blast was the result of an internal case of spontaneous combustion due to hot coal being placed in a bunker next to the magazine.

The initial assumption, however, was that the explosion was a Spanish act of war, and shortly thereafter, Congress appropriated $50 million to the war chest. The Spanish American War was declared on April 24, 1898. The battle cry was: "Remember the *Maine!*"

During the course of the war, *City of Washington* was used as a troop transport. The war was short, especially by today's standards, and came to an end with the signing of the Treaty of Paris on December 10, 1898. Under the treaty, the islands of Puerto Rico and Guam came under U.S. control and Spain gave up its claim to Cuba. It was also under this treaty that the United States was deeded use of Guantanamo Bay.

After the war, the *City of Washington* returned to its old business of shipping mail and passengers until its retirement from the

There were nearly 400 sailors aboard the *Maine* when it exploded while moored in Havana Harbor; the blast resulted in almost 300 casualties. Courtesy of Jerry Wilkinson Collection.

Hard and soft corals have become attached to the wreckage of the *City of Washington*. Courtesy of Florida Keys National Marine Sanctuary.

courier route in 1908. Three years later, it was sold to E. F. Luchenbach of New York, who gutted the ship and removed much of its superstructure and machinery.

The once-storied vessel was then relegated to the life of a coal barge. That is, at least, until July 10, 1917. On this particular day, three ships crashed into Elbow Reef. There was a tugboat, *Luchenbach #4*, *City of Washington*, and a barge called *Seneca*. The tugboat had been towing the *City of Washington* and the *Seneca* had been following close behind. Subsequently, the tugboat and the *Seneca* were refloated, and only the *City of Washington* succumbed to the reef's stony daggers.

Its remains were scattered over approximately 300 feet of the Atlantic bottom when the ship sank in 15 to 25 feet of water. The debris field is still evident. It includes sections of the keel and hull plates (with portholes) as well as a deck ladder and sections of the forward mast and propeller log shaft.

The wreck is visible from the surface, so snorkelers can see it without having to dive under.

However, what might not be clearly visible from the surface is the biodiversity attracted to the wreck site, as to every wreck site. These days, ships are purposefully sunk in order to create artificial reef sites, which is what all of these wrecks are. Shipwrecks provide structure, and underwater, structure acts as a beacon.

At a Glance

Name: *City of Washington*

How to get there: *City of Washington* is pretty common fare among the local charter trade for those snorkeling operations found in upper Key Largo. The wreck, found in 15 to 25 feet of water, is a brilliant piece of history, and for those wishing to see it firsthand, it is best to call ahead to find out which snorkeling outfits are visiting which sites on any given day. Most of the charter operations found between Mile Markers 106 and 95 frequent the wreck.

Weather and currents are always a factor, and like any operation out on the high seas, the final decision is always the captain's. For those with their own boats, it can be helpful to call one of the local charters to inquire about the conditions at the reef.

SNORKELING SITES

Reefs

Elbow Reef   GPS: 25 08.820N/ 80 15.190W; Depths: 10–35 feet

Shipwrecks

City of Washington   GPS: 25 08.786N/80 15.354W; Depths: 15–25
   feet

Fun Facts

Because corals are largely stationary, they rely on the warm, nutrient-rich waters of the Gulf Stream to deliver food. The current acts as a sort of neighborhood delivery service. Corals stick tiny tentacles out from their limestone houses in hopes of snagging "groceries" with the tips of their sticky tentacle fingers.

It is not, however, the only manner by which many corals gain sustenance. These corals also procure nutrients through a symbiotic relationship with zooxanthellae, tiny algae that take up residence inside the coral's house. These corals are by nature bone-colored organisms, and it is actually the zooxanthellae that give them color.

In a very real sense, zooxanthellae act as a living coat of paint. The coral gives the algae a place to live, and in return the algae lend it a colorful hue. The algae also provide nutrient-rich waste and oxygen. Sometimes, however, all of the zooxanthellae abandon a coral. The zooxanthellae bail out when they sense that the coral polyps are undergoing an inordinately high amount of stress due either to health or environmental issues.

This algal exodus is referred to as bleaching, because the colony loses its color. Like frogs in the terrestrial world, corals are significant indicator species in terms of assessing environmental health. Unfortunately, with rising water temperatures, pollution, and related human-driven contact, coral bleaching is an increasing threat to reefs around the world.

5

Molasses Reef

The nooks and crannies of Molasses Reef attract tropical fish like wildflowers draw honeybees. It is no wonder that the local charter trade refers to this site as the Aquarium. However, this moniker fails to capture just how impressive the reef really is.

The mix of sponges and corals creates a massive, brilliantly designed environment. Perhaps a more appropriate name would be "the Complex," as the reef seems more like a massive condominium complex than a mere aquarium. It is an absolute bio-magnet filled with an interesting mix of inhabitants.

Molasses Reef grows along the southernmost fringes of John D. Pennekamp Coral Reef State Park in 10 to 50 feet of clear turquoise water. A spur-and-groove reef formation, it is festooned with intricately designed hard corals, sponges shaped like barrels and vases, and supple soft corals like the brilliantly purple sea fan and delicate sea whip.

It is a popular destination for snorkelers and divers alike and, with 30 moorings buoys, the reef can become crowded—especially on weekends. In fact, it is widely thought that this is the most highly visited reef site along the Florida Reef.

How the reef got its particular name remains a bit of a mystery. Allegedly, it is derived from the wreck of a molasses transport that fell victim to these particular corals. Nothing seems to be written down in terms of corroborating evidence; no name(s) of a ship or ships or date(s) to substantiate a wreck seem to have been recorded.

Some accounts suggest the wreck involved a single molasses barge, while others say the name is the result of more than one wreck. The lone commonality is molasses, though in each and every case it is unclear whether or not the sweet, dark, viscous liquid ever seeped into the water.

It seems impossible that, with all the ships wrecking over the course of decades and decades in this vicinity, this one reef in particular—this well-developed, expansive reef—was given its proper credit so late. Odder still, perhaps, is that once it was named, the name's origin would be shady.

Interestingly, neighboring and smaller Pickles Reef and French Reef were established relatively early on by comparison. For instance, the *Amulet* is recorded as having struck Pickles Reef in 1831, and the *Yucatan* French Reef in 1847.

Clearly, long before the identifier stuck, the calcified branches of elkhorn corals were reaching for the Atlantic surface like stony daggers and impaling the odd ship. However, Molasses Reef was not so named until well after the Civil War. Of course, it does not help that reef identification in Florida's burgeoning years was not an exact science. Reef names were often confused, misspelled, and misidentified. It also did not help that for the first third of the nineteenth century, Key Largo reefs were nearly unilaterally referred to as Carysfort Reef, named for the 1770 wreck of the British warship, HMS *Carysfort*.

There are records of shipwrecks in the general vicinity that appear to have occurred in the appropriate time frame to inspire the viscous moniker Molasses Reef. They are not credited to Molasses

Reef, but it is possible that this is merely some kind of oversight. Two wrecks stand out in particular.

The first wreck occurred just to the north of Molasses Reef. The *Ben Cushing* left Havana and was bound for Portland with a load of molasses and cigars when it struck French Reef on February 22, 1862. The ship was lost, as was much of its cargo. The second ship struck to the south. The *Pauline* reportedly hit Pickles Reef on April 15, 1854, with a load of molasses and sugar. While the crew was rescued, the schooner and molasses were a total loss.

Even as late as 1868, Molasses Reef was not identified on conventional maps of the Florida Reef. Molasses is, after all, one of the larger reef structures in the entire barrier reef system. One of the first wrecks attributed to Molasses Reef did not hit the books until 1876, when the *Deodueus* met its fate on February 28 at 1:30 a.m. The British bark, under the command of Captain Peters, left Havana and was bound for Falmouth when it wrecked. It is from this point forward that shipwrecks began to be recorded as occurring on Molasses: *Energus* (1877), *Northhampton* (1883), and *Oxford* (1894).

Still, after a name finally stuck, it is not like the reef's history suddenly became illuminated. Molasses still has a little mystery hidden within its nooks and crannies. Largely, it involves debris found at a place on the reef locally referred to as the Winch Hole. Shipwreck debris has been collecting sponges, algae, and corals here for well over 100 years.

An ideal illustration of the historical confusion surrounding these reefs and the ships that wrecked upon them is the story of an Austrian ship that had been, on every account, loaded with cotton. According to Steven D. Singer's invaluable tome, *Shipwrecks of Florida*, the *Slabdova* reportedly left New Orleans in March of 1887 with a load of cotton literally stuffed into its holds. It is said to have struck French Reef on March 16.

In other records, on that very same day, March 16, 1887, another Austrian ship, *Slobodna*, delivering 4,500 bales of cotton from the docks of New Orleans to Europe's textile mills, reportedly wrecked on Molasses Reef. The confusion is likely one part misspelling and two parts reef misidentification, as evidence of the wreck is clearly visible at Molasses Reef.

The *Slobodna* had been constructed three years earlier on the island of Losinj, off the coast of what is today Croatia. The 1,100-ton, three-masted merchant vessel was iron framed with a wooden hull and is said to have struck Molasses Reef in 23 feet of water.

The ship became lodged on the coral, but it was not sinking. Problems arose, however, when the corals began to chisel away at the ship's wooden hull. As a result, water started to seep through the cracks and into the holds, and as it did, the cotton began to absorb the warm Atlantic water.

When cotton was transported in a ship's hold, it was literally jammed inside. To ensure that the maximum number of bales was squeezed into the available space, jackscrews were used to compress the bales. As such, the jammed-in bales on the *Slobodna* began to swell with water until the ship's distressed planks began to creak, moan, and split.

Pieces of the *Slobodna* still decorate the reef. There is not a whole lot of it still down there, though there are a few artifacts, including sections of the hull. Its three masts, too, lie across the sandy floor.

The ship's iron windlass was a steam-driven winch used to move the heavy chain attached to the ship's massive bow anchor. These days, the spot on the reef where that piece of equipment still sits is referred to as the Winch Hole and is a popular destination of the Key Largo charter trade.

Eventually, Molasses Reef was determined sufficiently hazardous and physically marked. In 1921, two identical unmanned lights

Queen angelfish at Molasses Reef. Photo by Krissy Gustinger.

were erected along the Florida Reef. One of the 45-foot-high iron structures was pounded into Pacific Reef, to the north in Biscayne National Park; the other was pounded into Molasses.

While both octagonal iron markers still stand out on their respective reefs, like headless horsemen, neither structure shoulders its light tower. With navigational advances and what was considered sufficient lighting from Carysfort and Alligator lighthouses, Molasses and Pacific reefs were deemed sufficiently lit and the light towers removed.

Unfortunately, none of the aforementioned markers proved alarming enough to the much-maligned (and for good reason) captain of the *Wellwood*. On August 4, 1984, the good captain ran his 400-foot vessel, its holds brimming with pelletized chicken feed, hard aground on the reef. The navigational miscalculation was a costly mistake for everyone and everything involved.

Like an apocalyptic deforestation, the hull of the *Wellwood* ground away nearly 20,000 square feet of coral reef until it was as smooth as the Overseas Highway. In total, nearly a quarter of a million square feet of brain coral, elkhorn coral, sea fans, sponges, and star coral were destroyed or injured. The resulting fine for habitat destruction was assessed at $6.275 million and the bill was paid over a 15-year period.

At a Glance

Name: Molasses Reef

How to get there: This spur–and–groove coral reef is one of the larger reefs in the chain and probably the most highly visited. It is equipped with 30 mooring buoys and can become quite crowded on weekends—especially holiday weekends. With depths ranging from 10 to 50 feet, the reef makes for excellent snorkeling. It is also easily accessible, as the reef is routinely visited by the charter industry from Pennekamp to Tavernier Creek, the pass separating Key Largo from Plantation Key, the next island in the chain. For those with their own boats, there is a public boat ramp at Harry Harris Park, MM 92.5.

SNORKELING SITES

Reefs

Molasses Reef   GPS: 25 00.579N/80 22.471W; Depths: 10–50 feet

Fun Facts

As a side note to the Molasses Light portion of the story, the head of the Pacific Reef Light can be found on dry land in Islamorada. The freshly painted light structure marks one of the two traffic turnabouts at Plantation Key's Founders Park (MM 87).

Perhaps it is now marking the excellent snorkeling right off the crescent-shaped beach at the park. Depths range from the beach to 5 feet. While this is no Molasses Reef, the hard-bottom coral community growing 20 yards off the southernmost tip of the cove is generally good for a surprise, be it a butterflyfish, seahorse, or even a manatee.

6

Pickles Reef

To see something a little different out at the reef, Pickles Reef is a one-of-a-kind excursion. Snorkelers will find the usual collection of sponges, elaborately configured corals, angelfish, and other assorted tropical fish. They will also have the opportunity to view an entirely different kind of structure, one that sets this small spur-and-groove reef formation apart from every other reef in the chain.

The reef is adorned with what were once pickle barrels, though the wooden barrels were not filled with dills or sweet gherkins. On the day they sank out at Pickles Reef, they were filled with mortar and being transported by a Civil War–era barge. The mortar was presumably to be used by Union forces for work on fortifications to the south—Fort Zachary Taylor, perhaps, or Fort Jefferson out at the Dry Tortugas.

The barrels must have sunk like woody bowling balls when seawater seeped inside and turned the mortar to cement. It took years for the wooden staves to rot away, but when they did, they left behind a concrete pickle barrel monument that looks like some kind of hillbilly decoration. The vessel that had been transporting the load, the Pickle Barrel Wreck, as the barge is referred to today, is proclaimed by many to be the origin of this reef's name.

Remarkably, it is not. Just how remarkable, however, is about to become clear. It is a reasonable theory that the name Pickles Reef was derived from the Pickle Barrel Wreck. But as it turns out, the name of the reef and the pickle barrel deposit are merely coincidental.

In reality, the reef had been known as Pickles Reef for a long time before the barrels ever came to rest at the bottom. In fact, Pickles Reef began to appear in the record books as early as 1828, decades before the first shots of the Civil War were ever fired. The odds must have been absolutely astronomical that a load of mortar-filled pickle barrels would sink at a reef already known as Pickles Reef!

Of course, the Pickle Barrel Wreck was not the only one to take place here. This shallow spur-and-groove reef formation growing in 10 to 30 feet of water has a pretty extensive history of shipwrecks. In fact, Key West Admiralty Court records identify 23 ships as having struck Pickles Reef between May of 1828 and May of 1911 (a few of which should, undoubtedly, be credited to nearby Molasses Reef). There have been other wrecks—certainly before 1828 and probably after 1911.

Because Pickles proved a fairly dangerous section of the reef, wreckers routinely patrolled the area. Though they suffered a poor reputation, wreckers were not bad fellows. In fact, Florida wreckers were by and large honest, hard-working sons of Neptune with a love for the sea and a job to do.

Wreckers were often the first responders on the scene of a shipwreck, and they braved inclement, even squally, weather to reach a ship in peril. In a manner of speaking, wreckers were the Coast Guard of their day. They were also licensed by the government and obligated to save the crew, the cargo, and, whenever possible, the ship.

Sketch of a Florida wrecker from J. B. Holder's "Along the Florida Reef," published in an 1871 edition of *Harper's New Monthly Magazine*. Courtesy of Jerry Wilkinson Collection.

If the wreckers failed to act in anything less than a professional capacity, the captain of the wrecked vessel, referred to, in the parlance of the day, as the master, could file a grievance before the judge at Key West's Admiralty Court.

Invariably, accounts from the master's point of view and those of the wreck master's, the captain in charge of the salvage operation, would differ. Should the wrecked ship's master prove eloquent enough to persuade the Key West magistrate, Judge Webb or Judge Marvin in later years, the wreck master could be punished for the crime of lack of effort. The judge could penalize the salvage reward and, in egregious scenarios, revoke a wrecker's license altogether.

Another of Holder's sketches from "Along the Florida Reef," showing wreckers trying to salvage a ship stuck on the reef. Courtesy of Jerry Wilkinson Collection.

While wreckers were, in most cases, hard-working, forthright men, like lawyers and used car salesmen, every industry cultivates the odd bad apple. The wrecking trade had Captain John Jacob Housman. Housman was, if not the most famous wrecker to ever work the Florida Reef, certainly the most infamous. When stories of crooked wreckers are told, Housman is usually involved. The brazen 26-year-old first hit the wrecking books in 1825 and would make his living from the reef, in one way or another, until his death in 1841.

The wreck of the *North Carolina* is an excellent example of wrecking at its absolute worst. Naturally, Captain Housman was involved. The ship hit Pickles Reef in 1832, and while Housman was not personally involved in the physical salvage of the schooner, he was part of a consortium of three wrecking captains involved in the operation.

What the consortium managed to salvage was the crew, the ship, and 366 bales of cotton. When it came time to discuss the bill, Captain Housman stepped forward. Housman talked the master of the *North Carolina* into forgoing the 90-mile trip to Key West to settle the matter before Judge Webb. Rather, he suggested it be settled through arbitration by an assembly of three impartial men on nearby Indian Key.

Technically, there were three approved ways to handle a salvage claim. Terms could be settled at sea, arbitrated back at the dock by an impartial party of three, or heard by Judge Webb in Key West's Wrecking Court. In the case of the *North Carolina*, the master agreed to move negotiations to the small wrecking community of Indian Key. He went so far as to enlist Housman as his business agent, a position that netted Housman an extra 5 percent of the negotiated salvage award.

Legally, the problem was not just that Captain Housman was part of the salvage consortium involving the ship he was representing. The bigger issue was that Indian Key was Housman's private wrecking paradise. He owned or had ownership in nearly every building on the 11-acre island and, thusly, had sway over every man negotiating the fair trade of goods for services.

As a result, like pirates balancing on a fence, the arbitrators awarded themselves 35 percent of the value of the salvaged schooner and its cargo—even though the going rate in Key West was 25 percent. To maximize their take, the arbitrators additionally undervalued the cotton at $20 per bale. Payment was rendered in the form of 122 bales of cotton, $100 in cash, and a debt of $600. Housman promptly sailed to Charleston and sold 50 of those bales of cotton for $50 each.

It was good he did it when he had the chance, because when Judge Webb got wind of the deal, he declared, "that the salvors, by their conduct, have forfeited all claim to compensation, even for services actually rendered" (Viele, *Florida Keys, vol. 3*, 147). Housman was made to turn over the remaining cotton bales.

Fortunately, history proves that Captain Housman turned out to be the exception, not the rule. At the other end of the spectrum is an incident on Pickles Reef involving Albert Koch. Koch was a German immigrant and self-taught paleontologist. Unlike the captain of the *North Carolina*, Professor Koch experienced the best of what the Florida wreckers had to offer.

The self-proclaimed doctor displayed what he could dig up or buy at his St. Louis museum; admission was fifty cents. The man was a little bit Robert Ripley and a little bit P. T. Barnum. In 1845, Koch was digging for fossils in the muddy waters of southwest Alabama's Sinatbouge Creek. While undoubtedly battling the advances of mosquitoes and alligators, Dr. Koch discovered what he claimed to be the remains of a monster.

The long-skulled and toothy skeleton was dug up, examined (unofficially), and named *Hydrargos sillimani*. The bones were packed into several crates, loaded onto a transport ship called the *Newark*, and shipped from Mobile, Alabama, to New York. It proved a bumpy ride. Squally weather was encountered in the Florida Straits, and the resulting high winds and heavy, pounding waves pushed the *Newark* onto Pickles Reef.

During the salvage operation, the crates containing Dr. Koch's bones were transferred from the *Newark* to a wrecking vessel.

The ship must have lurched when one of the crates slipped from a wrecker's grasp and into the drink. The wrecker tied the loose end of a rope to his vessel, grasped the other end in his tight-fisted hand, and dove overboard—proving that for at least some wreckers, the job was important.

The crate was recovered and the entire skeleton was ultimately delivered to New York. When the value of Koch's crates of bones was assessed, they were considered by the judge in Key West to be of historical and not monetary value. As such, their recovery did not factor into the salvage reward. Fortunately for those wreckers involved in the operation, there had also been cotton on board.

As for Koch's monster, it was later displayed at New York's Apollo Saloon, where Dr. Koch declared it, "without exception the largest of all fossil skeletons, found either in the old or new world . . . the blood thirsty monarch of the waters" must have measured "one hundred and forty feet" (Jones par. 21).

It was a fraud. The skeleton was actually an early predecessor of the modern whale called a Zeuglodon. Dr. Koch enhanced the skeleton by adding rib bones to lengthen it to 114 feet.

These days, aside from angelfish and the occasional loggerhead turtle, two things in particular make Pickles Reef an excellent snorkel. The pickle barrel monument as well as the remains of what is called the Pickle Barrel Wreck rest in 16 feet of water near the easternmost of the three mooring buoys helping to mark the reef.

The other really cool feature is pillar coral. At the northern end of the reef, pillar corals rise from the limestone substrate like, well, behemoth pickles. Perhaps the reason for the reef's odd name is that sailors of old saw what looked like pickles growing up toward the surface.

Perhaps Pickles Reef is really named after the stands of pillar corals growing there like behemoth pickles. Courtesy of Bill Brecht, Florida Keys National Marine Sanctuary.

At a Glance

Name: Pickles Reef

How to get there: This patch reef, found about 2 miles east of Tavernier Key, grows in 10 to 80 feet of water. Pickles Reef is another site readily visited by the local charter trade, though not generally by those operating near Pennekamp Park. To book a trip to this reef, contact charter outfits operating out of the Tavernier area. For those using their own transportation, there is a public boat ramp located at Harry Harris Park, Mile Marker 92.5, Oceanside (305-852-7161).

SNORKELING SITES

Reefs

Pickles Reef   GPS: 24 59.170N/80 24.940W; Depths: 10–80 feet

Fun Facts

One of the more interesting fish seen swimming at the reef is the parrotfish. Parrotfish have many distinguishing features. For one, their coloration is striking, for they are seemingly bejeweled in rich tropical hues. Also, parrotfish use their tails more as a rudder, like tail feathers, than as a means of locomotion. For that purpose, parrotfish flap their pectoral fins. Consequently, when they swim past, especially when they do so in great parrotfish schools, it looks like the brightly colored school is flying through the water.

However, it is not so much their striking scales or manner of locomotion that ultimately garnered this type of fish its avian name. Parrotfish are so named because of their teeth.

Parrotfish have mouths like beaks, and these beaks are perfectly suited to their dietary needs. The front teeth of a parrotfish are highly specialized—they use these teeth, these beaks, to take bites out of the coral reef. Should they be feeding in the vicinity, the noise, like celery being chomped, will be unmistakable.

Parrotfish feed on both the coral polyps living inside the limestone structure and the zooxanthellae, the colorful algae that live between the polyp and the limestone wall of its house. The limestone is ground up by another set of specialized teeth in the fish's throat, and the coral polyps and algae are digested.

The limestone passes through the fish's excretory system and is pooped out onto the ocean floor, creating piles of white sand. The sand is moved by the tides, and much of it washes up on shore. Parrotfish, in fact, are ultimately responsible for annually producing about one ton of sand per acre of coral reef.

7

Alligator Reef

Even to the casual observer, Alligator is one of the most visible Florida reefs. The spur-and-groove reef formation grows in 10 to 50 feet of water and is marked by an iron scarecrow. Because the massive iron structure punctuates the horizon like an exclamation mark, Alligator is also one of Islamorada's more asked-about reefs.

A popular snorkeling destination, the reef is frequently visited by the handful of charter boats operating in the area. Around the lighthouse, the seabed will be covered by a field of sea fans and vase sponges. Snorkelers will want to explore two basic areas, the lighthouse and the reef.

The water surrounding the lighthouse is about ten feet deep. While puddingwife wrasses, blue-headed wrasses, and damselfish will dart between the corals and sponges, a great deal of life can be observed under the lighthouse's shadow.

Expect barracudas to be floating under or near the lighthouse. While these snarly toothed, silvery torpedoes appear to be a fierce-looking lot, barracudas are largely curious fish that seem to make a habit of tagging along on snorkeling adventures. They mean no harm.

Painting of the U.S. schooner *Alligator* fighting pirates. Courtesy of Jerry Wilkinson Collection.

What should be made clear is that neither the lighthouse nor the reef were named for some reptile. In fact, the only confirmed alligator sighting on this particular reef was the U.S. schooner *Alligator*, a naval vessel specifically designed to combat pirates and slave traders. The 85-foot-long, maneuverable, double-masted schooner was once armed with a dozen cannons. With a draft of only 11 feet, it could give chase into relatively shallow waters.

The ship was built in the Boston Navy Yard and commissioned in March of 1821. It was assigned to the West Indies Squadron and subsequently sent to fight piracy in the West Indies and the Florida Straits. While its life was storied, it was not very long.

The *Alligator* was captained by Lieutenant William H. Allen. The following year, 1822, it was moored off the northern coast of

Cuba. Pirate hunting had been slow, and the captain and his crew of fighting marines had been slowly growing restless. The general state of malaise that had settled over the ship, however, was about to be shaken off.

While in port, the ship was approached by two American merchant marines who regaled Lt. Allen with a pirate tale of how their ship, the *Anna Maria,* along with its load of molasses, had been taken by a crew of pirates and was being held 42 miles to the east for a $7,000 ransom.

The *Alligator's* crew of 9 officers and 45 men were quick to take action, and they sailed the 42 miles east to rescue the ship. The *Anna Maria* was being held in a cove, but it was not alone. A handful of captured ships were being held and guarded by the pirate ship *Revenge.* The intrepid marines and sailors of the *Alligator* wasted no time in attacking.

The gunfire exchange was heard by another pirate schooner anchored nearby. The second pirate schooner entered the fray. The *Alligator's* marines and sailors were outnumbered by 100 pirates, but they fought on. Five men from the *Alligator* were wounded and at least 2 killed. Lt. Allen was wounded twice and died about 4 hours later. Most of the crew of the *Revenge* escaped alive, but they did so without their ship.

The *Anna Maria* and the rest of the captives were liberated, and Lieutenant John M. Dale took command of the *Alligator.* His first mission was to escort the convoy from its Cuban anchorage to Norfolk, Virginia. The problem was that while the *Alligator* was built for speed, much of the convoy, the *Anna Maria* in particular, was built for capacity. It did not take long for the merchant ship and its load of molasses to fall behind.

Lt. Dale ordered the *Alligator* to slow its speed, which required tacking back and forth in the dangerous Florida Straits. At approximately 9:30 p.m. on November 22, 1822, the *Alligator* slammed into the Florida Reef. It hit hard, and while the crew tried for a couple of days to work the ship off the reef, the vessel could not be dislodged. In the following days, the *Anna Maria* was sighted, and the crew of the *Alligator* attracted their attention with gunfire. The tackle, weapons, and cargo were stripped from the *Alligator* and stowed on the *Anna Maria*. Rather than leave the wreckage behind for pirates to scavenge, Lt. Dale and several of his men set fire to the schooner and presumably watched as it exploded. Suffice it to say that little remains of the U.S. schooner *Alligator*.

It is the obvious namesake of one of the earliest marked reefs in the chain. Alligator Reef was 1 of 15 reefs initially marked with iron posts topped with black barrels by Assistant of the Coast Survey Francis Gerdes in 1849.

In 1857, the Light-House Board recommended a series of iron lighthouses to mark the reef line so that it would become "as perfectly lighted as it is believed any capable and intelligent mariner could desire. In a distance of three hundred miles there will then be Dry Tortugas, Sand Key, Dry Bank (Sombrero Reef), Alligator Reef, Carysfort Reef, Cape Florida, and Sebastian Inlet seacoast lights."

Initial plans for a light to be erected at Alligator Reef were put on hold when the Civil War erupted. Plans for the project were shelved until Congress once again allocated the necessary funds in 1870. The iron pile lighthouse still guarding the reef today was forged by Paulding Kemble of Cold Springs, New York, and shipped, in parts and pieces, to nearby Indian Key.

Indian Key was chosen as a staging ground for the light's erection because the island was equipped with a fairly deep harbor and had a reputation for remaining relatively mosquito-free. Out at the reef, workers were leveling a sufficient swath of coral reef to arrange nine massive iron disks in an octagonal formation on the limestone substrate to serve as a structural base. The iron

An aerial image of Indian Key showing the former town square and roads. Courtesy of Jerry Wilkinson Collection.

screw-pile supports were then driven 10 feet into the coral by a 2,000-pound hammer lifted by a steam-powered pile driver, one inch at a time.

Alligator Lighthouse was completed in 1873 at a cost of $185,000. The manned outpost stood 136 feet high and bore a light visible for 18 miles. The keeper's quarters consisted of 4 rooms with double doors, 2 bedrooms, a kitchen, living room, and an enclosed spiral staircase leading up to the light. George R. Billberry was the first keeper.

Under the Presidential Reorganization Act of 1939, Alligator Lighthouse, in fact all U.S. lighthouses, were integrated into the U.S. Coast Guard. It remained a manned station until its automation in 1963. Today it alerts passing vessels to the nearby reef the same way it did in 1873. The big difference now is that the light is home to a fleet of cormorants and a squadron of barracudas that patrol the shallow turquoise waters beneath it.

Jim Clupper, a former librarian at the Helen Wadley Branch of the Monroe County Library, suggests that one of the earliest Islamorada libraries was actually Alligator Lighthouse. Clupper, a researcher and historian responsible for the remarkable Florida Room, a treasure trove of local history at the Islamorada branch, came upon a letter during one of his forays into history that was written in 1913 by the Bureau of Lighthouses. It stated, "Traveling book collections—crates that converted to book shelves—were provided to lighthouse keepers and crews, who were discouraged from reading trashy novels."

The observation mirrors an account written by Kirk Munroe and published in 1898.

A reef lighthouse is always well supplied with the latest novels, magazines, and papers by New York steamers that pass close to it every day. A keeper puts out from the light in a small boat.

The mate of an approaching steamer has already collected such paper, magazines and novels as the passengers are willing to spare, done them up in a bundle, and tied them to a billet of wood. As the steamer passes the waiting boat, the package is tossed overboard. The lighthouse man waves his thanks, captures the dripping prize, and carries it back to his iron dwelling, where its contents are sorted and dried. (Munroe 89)

Lighthouse keepers were also there to watch over the reefs. When they observed a wreck, they would raise a flag as a call for assistance. In 1919, Assistant Keeper Richard C. Richards was on watch when he witnessed a seaplane crash 10 miles from Alligator Light. Reportedly, he immediately launched the lighthouse boat and sped out to the wreck site. The Bureau of Lighthouses praised Richards in its report, stating that he "dived into shark-infested waters to locate the 2 men in the plane" (Dean 215).

Snorkelers should not let that quote scare them; these are not shark-infested waters. They are, however, excellent snorkeling waters. Alligator Reef is one of the largest individual reef tracts in the entire barrier reef chain. It is also a Sanctuary Preservation Area, so there is no harvesting of anything living or dead within the boundaries of the four large yellow marking buoys.

The remains of the U.S. schooner *Alligator* can be found between the lighthouse and the reef line to the east. There is not much to see of the wreck, just some piles of ballast stones that, to the casual observer, began to look much like every other part of the reef a long time ago.

During a fish count at specific sites along the reef in the 1960s, Alligator Reef recorded the highest number of individual species—over 500—that could be attributed to a single reef site. While it might prove difficult to identify 500 individual species out at the reef today, it is still populated by a host of tropical fish, including parrotfish, damselfish, gobies, and angelfish.

The reef is an excellent snorkel. While the substrate near the lighthouse is largely home to soft coral and sponges, the hard corals, such as star and brain corals, grow up from the reef just to the east. The reef is a brilliant canvas for everything that is so great about these waters.

Slip into the waters, greet the barracudas under the lighthouse, and remember that while they look sinister, they are curious creatures, not menacing ones.

At a Glance

Name: Alligator Reef

How to get there: Alligator Reef is a spur-and-groove reef formation growing in 10 to 50 feet of water about 3.5 miles southeast of the southern tip of Upper Matecumbe Key. For those snorkelers towing their own boats, there is a public boat ramp located on Indian Key Fill, Mile Marker 77, Bayside.

Two charter boat outfits in the area generally frequent Alligator: Bud and Mary's, and the Happy Cat, which departs out of Robbie's Marina. Key Dives operates out of Bud and Mary's (MM 80) and caters generally to scuba divers, though certainly welcomes snorkelers. The only charter in the area catering specifically to snorkelers is the Happy Cat, operating out of Robbie's Marina (MM 77.5).

Another excellent snorkeling site located near Alligator Reef is Cheeca Rocks (GPS: 24 54.245N/80 36.885W). The near-shore patch reef is located about one mile off the beach of the Cheeca Lodge (MM 82). It grows in 3 to 15 feet of water and is festooned with a pretty fantastic collection of mountainous star and brain corals, a scattering of staghorn coral structures, and the ubiquitous purple sea fan. It has lots of fish, too, including butterflyfish, wrasses, and elegant angelfish. Cheeca Rocks is regularly visited by the aforementioned Happy Cat.

SNORKELING SITES

Reefs

Alligator Reef   GPS: 24 51.779N/80 37.339W; Depths: 8–50 feet
Cheeca Rocks   GPS: 24 54.245N/80 36.885W; Depths: 3–15 feet

Fun Facts

For those who have not been followed by a barracuda, the experience can be unnerving. Intrepid snorkelers will turn and give the fish a taste of its own medicine. Swim in the barracuda's direction, not aggressively, and odds are the fish will turn and swim away.

8

Indian Key

Not every excellent snorkeling opportunity in the Florida Keys is out at the reef. Some can be found much closer to shore, like Indian Key. At first glance, the island sits seemingly inconsequentially in the Atlantic shallows between Upper and Lower Matecumbe Keys. This island, however, deserves a closer look.

From the Lignumvitae Channel Bridge at Mile Marker 77, the island looks like another stray, undeveloped Florida key. It is not. This fascinating almost-11-acre island represents not just another snorkeling site, but a bona fide snorkeling adventure.

What is not readily apparent about Indian Key is that, once upon a time, it was the second most developed community in the island chain (after Key West). Not only is Indian Key a storied ghost town and a state park, but abutting it is an excellent hard-bottom coral community.

Elegant stands of coral do not grow in the shallows surrounding the island. Rather, snorkelers will encounter two distinctly different inshore environments—the aforementioned hard-bottom coral community and seagrass beds. Rich, emerald fields of seagrass surround about half of the island. Granted, seagrass beds are not the most exciting snorkeling destination, but there is always the chance of swimming over a pink-lipped conch or a blood-orange cushion star.

Keep in mind, however, that life in a seagrass field is not always so easy to distinguish. In fact, often it is quite subtle. Camouflage is a proven survival technique and can mean the difference between life and death. To make the most out of a seagrass snorkeling experience, it is important to spend time floating. What might at first glance appear to be a single blade of grass moving with the tide could actually be a seahorse.

The other environment half-surrounding Indian Key is what is referred to as a hard-bottom coral community. These are areas of the seafloor, generally found close to shore, where seagrass beds share the substrate with a mix of sponges, rocky outcroppings, and a concentrated sprinkling of both soft and stony corals.

The Atlantic side of Indian Key is decorated thusly, with a sampling of vase sponges, slimy sea feathers, and at least one low-profile brain coral the color of a key lime. Make no mistake, like their offshore counterparts, these near-shore sites also attract a host of fish, conchs, and lobster. Part of what makes these near-shore sites so exciting is that there really is no telling what species might reveal itself at any given time. A manatee could even show up!

Mature snappers and grunts school abundantly here, as well as a pretty cast of juvenile tropical fish such as wrasses, tangs, and surgeonfish. Look closely and you will see bumblebee-patterned sergeant majors no bigger than the nail on a pinky finger. At high tide, the snappers, grunts, and parrotfish can be found schooling right up to the jagged edges of the island.

However, the snorkeling is only half of the Indian Key experience. Indian Key is a ghost town of sorts. Take time to explore the old road system on the island—it is still intact. The island used to host a thriving community. To begin the story, the island was not always called Indian Key.

Two of the first recorded names associated with the island are Cayuelo de Matanza and French Key. Cayuelo de Matanza, roughly translated from its Spanish origins, means Little Slaughter Key. This refers to the plight of a group of French sailors once reputed to have been shipwrecked on the island. They were slaughtered by local Indians, spurring the genesis of both of these early names.

The old Bahamian sailors used to call it Cay Comfort because the island is located roughly midway along the Florida Reef. Another reason for this particular name was its reputation for being relatively mosquito-free. Freshwater, too, could be found on nearby Lower Matecumbe Key.

The first recorded use of the name Indian Key was in 1775, when cartographer Bernard Romans noted the island on his map as both Matanza and Indian Key. Ironically, the name Indian Key in no way references the singular event that the island is most infamous for.

Of course it is impossible to talk about Indian Key and not bring up Captain John Jacob Housman, the Wrecker King of Indian Key. One of nine children, he was born on Staten Island, New York, in 1799. An intrepid sailor, he was appointed captain of his father's 56-foot schooner, *William Henry*, at an early age. It did not take long, however, for the sailor to set his sights on more tropical latitudes. By his early twenties, the young captain was navigating the treacherous Florida Straits.

Young Captain Housman promptly sailed his schooner onto a coral reef. The *William Henry* was refloated by a local wrecking crew and hauled to Key West for repair. As Captain Housman waited, he observed the intricate dance of captains, dock workers, and merchants whenever wrecks were brought to port.

It soon became apparent to him that the wrecking industry had its fingers in everybody's pockets. Key West was a consortium and, recognizing a monopoly when he saw one, Captain Housman hatched his grand idea. Once the *William Henry* was shipshape, Housman entered into the Key West wrecking game.

Housman is one of the most infamous wreckers of the era, and he managed to earn a reputation in pretty short order. Contrary to popular opinion, history has shown that wreckers were basically well mannered and hardworking, and the industry itself was a pretty straightforward enterprise, with differences settled in court. What made Captain Housman stand out was that, while he repeatedly proved himself a capable captain who could obviously get things done, he was also of dubious character.

After a couple of years operating out of Key West, Housman took the wealth he had accumulated (some would say surreptitiously) and relocated his wrecking operation north to Indian Key. He chose the island for three reasons: it was Cay Comfort, it was just beyond the oversight of Key West, and it was already fairly established when he arrived in 1830.

The first white settler, Silas Fletcher, had come to the island in 1824 aboard a schooner stocked with goods, under orders to build a store. He proceeded to build a two-story home for his family, and once they arrived, a handful of wreckers and turtlers followed, building homes and establishing families.

By the time Housman arrived, the community was over a dozen families strong. Housman, however, was the man responsible for developing the island, designing a street system and town square as well as building wharves, docks, a large warehouse, and shops for sailmakers, carpenters, clerks, and a blacksmith.

He also spent a small fortune landscaping the island (a reported $40,000, a huge sum at the time!)—importing fertile topsoil, fruit trees, tropical plants, and flowering shrubs. Indian Key was flour-

Artist rendering of how Indian Key was thought to have looked in the 1830s. Courtesy of Jerry Wilkinson Collection.

ishing. By 1832, in fact, the wharves were generating sufficient commerce to qualify for an inspector of customs.

The following year, the United States Post Office established Indian Key Station, and Silas Fletcher, a man who wore many hats in the community, became Indian Key's first postmaster. He was also the island's first justice of the peace. At that time, the only other post office in the archipelago was in Key West.

It was the outbreak of the Second Seminole War in 1835 that put a damper on island living. The Indians, once frequent traders on the island, were being chased down, hunted, and killed. They were fighting for their existence, and Indian Key was this little island out in the middle of nowhere that, while well provisioned, was poorly guarded. For the families still calling the island home, tensions became palpable.

Captain Housman petitioned the government for military support, but received no timely response. Decisions had to be made, as safety was becoming a serious issue. So Captain Housman organized Company B, 10th Regiment of the Florida Patrol, and declared himself captain. He paid the daily wage of the outfit from his own pocket (30 cents a day, plus another 50 cents for rations), and also ordered the island be fortified. He strategically placed four cannons around the island. As a reminder to any force that might be lurking and plotting, one cannon was fired every day.

Housman was fighting wars on other fronts as well. What he wanted most was to not have to answer to Key West officials. In his perfect world, Housman wanted Indian Key to be its own sovereign entity. After several official petitions to separate Key West from Indian Key, the argument that finally swayed officials was the declaration that citizens of the northern reaches of Monroe County underwent undue hardships when called to serve jury duty in Key West.

Key West officials were summarily enraged when they learned that, on February 4, 1836, Monroe County had been divided into two. All keys east of Bahia Honda were now considered part of Dade County. The county seat was assigned, albeit temporarily, to Indian Key. To help cement the appointment, Housman built a courthouse on the island.

Help on the Indian front would not arrive until a Revenue Marine schooner, under Navy orders, showed up in 1838. Much to Captain Housman's chagrin, the Revenue Marines bypassed Indian Key and set up their makeshift fort, Fort Paulding, on nearby Tea Table Key. In any case, tensions seemed to be assuaged by the military presence, and Company B disbanded.

There was a return to normalcy in the community. In fact, in January of 1840, an advertisement for Indian Key's Tropical Hotel read: "A large and convenient house has recently been opened on Indian Key, to be known as the Tropical Hotel and where invalids and others traveling for health or pleasure will find convenient

Portrait of Lt. John McLaughlin. Courtesy of Jerry Wilkinson Collection.

and comfortable quarters, good fare, attentive servants, and moderate charge."

The resort hotel, one of the first in the island chain, featured a 9-pin bowling alley, a billiard table, and a popular bar—all owned by Captain Housman. Life on the island, however, would take a turn for the worse when Lt. John McLaughlin arrived with his Florida Squadron and took command of Fort Paulding.

His strategy to fight the Indians was to withdraw forces from around all the keys and mount one major offensive into the Everglades. When he did so, however, he took all but a handful of his forces, and Fort Paulding was virtually abandoned. A total of five men were left behind to tend the sick and wounded.

In the meantime, Chief Chekika and more than 100 warriors were hiding behind the Matecumbe mangroves, waiting for the Navy to make its move. It was approximately 2:00 a.m. on August 7, 1840, when the Indians attacked. The attack constituted one of the few documented instances where an Indian war party crossed a body of water to attack.

The general store, homes, and businesses of Indian Key were looted and burned, and, of the roughly 50 inhabitants, 10 were killed, wounded, or captured. Many of the island's residents ran into the water, splashing and jumping and swimming to get away. Captain Housman and his wife, too, retreated to the warm Atlantic shallows. Unfortunately, two of the family's large dogs followed— when the dogs began to bark excitedly, Housman was forced to drown the hounds with his bare hands to avoid revealing their position.

Lieutenant Commander McLaughlin penned his official account of the Indian Key raid to J. K. Paulding, secretary of the Navy, while aboard the U.S. schooner *Flirt* on August 11, 1840. Part of the letter read, "approximately 134 Indians leaving in 34 boats, six taken from Indian Key." He listed the dead as Dr. Perrine, Mr. Matte, his wife, and two young children, and a "lad named Lindy, drowned in a cistern where he hid." Mr. Otis was described as wounded. "Missing are a negro woman with two children carried off by the Indians."

With the island all but destroyed, Captain Housman signed the property over to McLaughlin and returned to Key West, where he found work on a wrecking vessel, though not as captain. McLaughlin relocated Fort Paulding to Indian Key and spent $10,000 rebuilding damaged cisterns and some of the existing structures. A hospital was constructed, as were barracks and storehouses.

Meanwhile, back in Key West, while working a wreck in rough

seas, Housman was crushed to death between the hulls of two ships. Lore suggests that his widow brought the body back to Indian Key and interred it in the coral bedrock. However, local historian Jerry Wilkinson is quick to point out the lack of evidence supporting this story. While the rather significant marble tombstone she commissioned in his honor was deposited on the island, there is no definitive proof it ever marked his actual grave.

What is clear is that McLaughlin's Florida Squadron abandoned Fort Paulding in rather short order. When Housman's former clerk, Walter C. Maloney, came back to survey the island in 1843, it was reported deserted. Subsequently, Indian Key was sold at public auction on the steps of the Key West County Courthouse for $355. The island did not remain deserted for long.

Dr. J. B. Holder visited the archipelago in the 1860s and documented his adventure for *Harper's Magazine*. Indian Key seems to have been experiencing a revival. He had this to say about the island:

> The grand rendezvous for the wreckers fortunately for us was near at hand. Indian Key is one of the few islands of the Reef that can be called inhabited. Here for many years the wreckers have resorted, as it is convenient as a midway station and the safest harbor in heavy weather. The whole island seems to have been under cultivation. Fine cocoa palms and many flowering shrubs are here, and what with the several houses the place looks quite village-like and picturesque.

One of the men living on the island at the time, according to the 1860 U.S. Census, was Charles Goodyear. Charles Goodyear patented the process of vulcanizing rubber and is the namesake of Goodyear Tires. By 1870, the Pinders, a familiar name around Islamorada still, were farming bananas on the island.

Indian Key was also chosen as a staging area for the assembly of Alligator Light in 1873. It seems that the island once again diminished in the following years. This explains why Key West Union forces used the island as a hospital detachment named Camp Bell two years later. The isolated hospital operated from April 3 to October 29 during a Key West yellow fever epidemic. Once Camp Bell collapsed its tents and moved on, life on Indian Key dried up again. While the post office operated and disbanded from time to time, depending on population, Indian Key Station closed once and for all in 1880. What took place on the island in the years to follow is anyone's guess, though it is reported that during Prohibition the island was used as a waypoint for rumrunners transporting liquor between the Bahamas and Miami.

The island was being utilized as a fish camp on Labor Day weekend in 1935. Like the rest of Islamorada, Indian Key was devastated by the Great Labor Day Hurricane, the most powerful hurricane ever recorded in the United States. After the storm, Ernest Hemingway, who was living in Key West at the time, packed his boat, *Pilar*, with emergency supplies and motored north to Islamorada. "Indian Key absolutely swept clean, not a blade of grass, and over the high center of it were scattered live conchs that came in with the sea, craw fish, and dead morays," he wrote. "The whole bottom of the sea blew over it" (Baker 422).

The state bought the island and designated it Indian Key Historic State Park in 1971. While many of the island's historical remains have succumbed to vandals and treasure hunters, it is a fascinating place to explore, above and below the surface. Pack a picnic. Bring shoes to stroll the island. Sometimes, in summer months, thousands of fairy green butterflies cloud the air.

The street system is still intact, and what remains is basically a ghost town with placards explaining which ruins are what. A replica of Captain Housman's massive gravestone is on display at what can only be the supposed place of his burial. More than likely, this is not his actual burial site.

Ernest Hemingway aboard his ship, *Pilar*. Courtesy of Jerry Wilkinson Collection.

When it comes to exploring the shallows surrounding the island, snorkelers should remember, while they are marveling at the corals and damselfish, that residents of Indian Key once waded, splashed, and swam through these same shallows in their attempt to escape the invading Indians.

The best snorkeling is on the eastern side of the island; start at the dock and swim around this edge of the key.

While conch and lobster are fairly frequently spotted in these shallows, Indian Key is considered a Sanctuary Preservation Area of the Florida Keys National Marine Sanctuary, and the harvesting of items, living or dead, is prohibited. It is important to realize that this is a fragile environment especially vulnerable to the inadvertent maiming caused by unwieldy fins. Without realizing it, snorkelers can be as destructive as Godzilla on a stroll through downtown Tokyo. So, when you visit, be a conscientious monster.

At a Glance

Name: Indian Key
Web site: http://www.floridastateparks.org/indiankey/default.cfm
How to get there: While this historic piece of real estate is not accessible by automobile, it is easily reached by boat or kayak. Kayakers can launch from Tea Table Fill (Mile Marker 78). For those without their own kayaks, Robbie's Marina (Mile Marker 77.5) is home to Florida Keys Kayak, better known around the property as the Kayak Shack. John and his crew have everything necessary for the paddle to Indian Key.

For kayakers, the biggest problem with the 25-minute paddle from the tarpon-riddled waters surrounding the dock at Robbie's is that paddling wrinkles the turquoise Atlantic blanket covering the beautiful, emerald beds of seagrass separating Lower Matecumbe from Indian Key.

Sometimes the seagrass flats will appear deserted, and sometimes pink-lipped conch or blood-orange Bahamian sea stars will show up. Sometimes sharks patrol the flats—small bonnetheads or nurse sharks. Depths around Indian Key range from 1 to 8 feet.

SNORKELING SITES

Along the east side of the island.

Fun Facts

Back before the attack on Indian Key, one of the men stationed at Fort Paulding, on Tea Table Key, was Midshipman Edward Zane Carroll Judson. Judson's life reads much like Ernest Hemingway's, though Judson arrived nearly a century before Hemingway set foot on Florida's most famous archipelago.

Still, the two men were brothers of a sort; their passions included war, women, and fighting. Midshipman Judson was said to have been challenged to a fight by 13 sailors, who he agreed to fight one by one. Some were reportedly knocked out, and some were battered and bruised, and the rest, so the story goes, left him alone.

It has been widely noted that Midshipman Judson was prone to exaggeration. The man served in the Navy until 1842, afterwards traveling West, where he made friends with a few American icons. Judson might better be remembered by his pen name, Ted Buntline. Ted Buntline was once considered not only the most popular, but one of the wealthiest writers in America.

The dime store novelist was the first to serialize the exploits of Buffalo Bill Cody. He also did a little writing about John Housman, who might owe at least a portion of his reputation to Buntline's popular version of Captain Housman's exploits, "Sketches of the Florida War," published in the *Pensacola Gazette* on March 29, 1845.

About Indian Key, he wrote that Captain Housman "spent such care upon its improvements, that it soon became a miniature Eden." About the captain personally, he wrote, "Wrecks came rapidly and as his purse swelled, his importance likewise extending. He took great care to let none except those who were subservient to his will, reside upon the island, thus literally making himself a monarch of all he surveyed. Housman, after his return from Charleston, was doubly successful in his calling, and his property rapidly increased on the one hundred thousand principal three or four times multiplied."

He also wrote about the infamous Indian attack, of which he said, "The attacking party was led by Chico and Chikika, two celebrated and bloody chiefs. They were supposed to consist of from two hundred to two hundred and fifty to three hundred in number."

9

Coffins Patch Reef

The Middle Keys do not attract the same attention as Key Largo, Islamorada, and Key West. Visitors tend to view Marathon as a place to pass through, stopping only to fuel up or take a bathroom break on their way to or from Key West.

With the likely exception of Grassy Key's Dolphin Research Center, this particular stretch of the archipelago has never really established a vacation-destination identity, or even the reputation for a great margarita. For snorkelers, this is a best-case scenario: the reefs here have escaped the deluge of visitors that their northern and southern counterparts have endured. It is truly a good thing.

There is some excellent snorkeling between Duck and Vaca Keys, and Coffins Patch Reef is a prime example. This is sort of a misnomer, as it is not a single, shallow-patch reef, but a collection of six reef sites stretching out across the Atlantic substrate for more than a mile. Generally speaking, each individual patch reef grows in 10 to 30 feet of water.

The common thread linking them together seems to be a blend of elegant stands of brain and pillar corals, soft slimy sea feathers, and large barrel sponges that attract schools of goat fish, grunts, and yellowtail snappers. These particular coral gardens also seem to be a haven for butterflyfish. The reefs, too, are a treasure trove of history.

Let us start with Juan Ponce de León's intrepid expedition of 1513, which took the Spaniard to the New World and back again. The map he created along the way would chart the course followed by a seemingly endless train of Spanish treasure fleets. For hundreds of years to come, merchant ships would sail from Spain to Vera Cruz, Mexico, where, one by one, they would be filled with New World treasures, silver, and gold.

When the loading was done, the ships sailed from Vera Cruz to Cuba, where the fleet would reconvene in Havana Harbor, a Spanish-held port. It was here that the ships were given final provisioning before leaving for the dangerous trip through the unpredictable Florida Straits, past the Florida Reef, and home again.

On July 13, 1733, 16 fully loaded merchant vessels of the New Spain Fleet departed Havana Harbor, sailing home to deliver their booty to the king of Spain. The treasure ships were given a military escort led by Lieutenant General Don Rodrigo de Torres aboard the 60-gun warship, *El Rubi* (also known as the *Capitana*). His command was augmented by three secondary military vessels, and two of them, the *Almiranta El Gallo Indiana* and the *Refuerzo El Infante*, were also 60-gun warships.

Additionally, the fleet was accompanied by two smaller ships carrying supplies to the presidio of St. Augustine. It would not be smooth sailing for the 22 ships that left port that morning. Two days into the voyage, Naval Commissioner Don Alonso Herrera Barragan wrote a letter to the president of the Council of Trade at Cadiz from aboard the *Capitana El Rubi*.

The 14th we discovered the land of the Keys of Florida. At 9:00 that night the wind began to rise out of the North. It continued to freshen to the point where we all knew a hurricane was imminent. We found ourselves close to the expressed Keys, with the wind and seas so strong we were unable to govern ourselves, and each new gust came upon us with renewed major force. On the 15th, signs were made (among the ships of the fleet) to try to arrive back in Havana, but we were unable to do so for the wind went around to the South without slacking its force or lessening the seas. By 10:30 that night we had all grounded in the expressed Keys at a distance of 28 leagues in length.

Despite the hurricane, four ships managed to return to Havana. In addition, *El Africa* (according to some sources also called the *San Jose*) survived the hurricane with minimal damage—the loss of a topmast and some rigging—and was able to find safe anchorage near Key Largo. Repairs were made in the following days, and it managed to cross the Atlantic and deliver its treasures to the king.

The rest of the fleet was less fortunate. Seventeen ships were wrecked, sunk, or destroyed, and the carnage of fallen masts, splintered planks, treasures, and drowned bodies was spread along the Florida Reef for 80 miles, from Key Biscayne to Vaca Key.

One of the ships lost in the storm was the *San Ignacio*, an English-built ship that displaced 292 tons and had a crew, at least on this trip, of 52. Among its cargo were 12,000 pesos in silver specie and bullion, 696 *marcos* of worked silver, and china from the Far East. The *San Ignacio* broke apart and scattered its treasure when it struck a series of patch reefs off of Vaca Key. That reef system is now called Coffins Patch Reef. Fourteen men survived the ordeal.

A second ship is reported to have succumbed to the Coffins Patch Reef as well, *El Floridano*, leaving one survivor. Those who did manage to survive gathered on nearby islands, made camps, and waited for help to arrive.

Help was not long in coming. When Spanish admiralty officials in Cuba got wind of the imperiled treasure fleet, 9 rescue ships equipped with supplies, food, divers, and salvage equipment left Havana for the wreck sites.

Once the rescue fleet arrived, 3 of the wrecked ships were re-floated and sailed back to Havana. The rest of the fleet was salvaged—very successfully salvaged. It took a couple of years to complete, but when all the recovered New World treasures were tallied up, the Spaniards reclaimed more silver, gold, and china from the shipwrecks than were originally claimed on the fleet's cargo manifests! Much of the extra booty had been treasures smuggled by sailors and unscrupulous captains.

The reef where the *San Ignacio* and *El Floridano* reportedly wrecked is located about 3.5 miles southeast of Key Colony Beach, at the Coffins Patch Reef. The name is a bastardization of an earlier English name. It seems that the reef was originally called Collins Patches Reef, "after the captain of a vessel who was wrecked there (there is only 5 feet of water on it)" (Gerdes 48).

There are multiple accounts of shipwrecks in this area at a reef called Collins Patches. One of them was the bark called *Othello*, which reportedly struck Collins Patches Reef on March 14, 1832. In a second account, the *New York Times* reported that, on February 12, 1853, the English bark *Colony*, sailing from New Orleans to London, wrecked on Collins Patches Reef on February 2.

Things changed, however, sometime in the 1850s, because by 1856, the reef was being identified as Coffin's Patches Reef. Coffin's Patches was 1 of 15 reefs marked by Lieutenant James Totten of the U.S Army during his inspection of the Florida Reef. Each chosen site was marked with a 36-foot iron day marker erected on a screw-pile foundation and topped with a black barrel.

Coffin's Patches was also the original site chosen for what would become the Sombrero Key Lighthouse. In fact, work had started on the construction of the 160-foot-high iron structure, but the work platform was destroyed by a hurricane on August 29, 1856, and further construction plans were put on hold.

After the destruction of the previous year's hurricane, plans for the light were reassessed, and ultimately it was decided to relocate the light to its current position at Sombrero Reef, 9 miles to the south. Sombrero Reef was also referred to as Dry Bank because of the spit of land that used to be there. In 1857, the United States Light-House Board issued a statement announcing, "The most important light-house structures underway in this district are the Dry Bank (near Coffin's patches) light-house; . . . and the first class masonry tower at Dry Tortugas" (Dean 304).

There is an alternative story about how the reef was named. This fun, spooky story occasionally floated around is that the current name, Coffins Patch Reef, is the result of a cargo ship hauling wood coffins wrecking on the reef. While the image of wood coffins floating over the corals like Dracula's regatta is wildly entertaining, it never happened.

Additionally, while it is true that evidence of the 1733 treasure fleet remains along the Florida Reef, after nearly 300 years, little to none is left at the Coffins Patch reefs. Rest assured, however, that the shallow coral heads adorning this series of reefs have more than enough to keep a snorkeler interested.

The patch most often visited by the local charter trade is called the Stake. This name refers to an iron beam that juts out of the water like the limb of a rusty skeleton. One myth claims this piece of metal is the remnant of a lighthouse destroyed by a hurricane in 1935.

There are, however, many legitimate theories regarding the stake's origin. It could be what remains of the 36-foot marker erected by Totten and the Coast Survey men back in 1856. Then again, it could also have been left behind by Flagler's men during construction of the Oversea Railroad. One explanation is that it is the remnant of a shipwreck.

In any case, the Stake, as the site is now referred to, is the most widely visited of the Coffins Patch reefs. This particular reef is a

Branching corals like this stand of elkhorn coral have been a nightmare for ships since captains first attempted navigating the Florida Straits, especially for those sailing past shallow reefs like Coffins Patch Reef. Courtesy of Todd Hitchins, Florida Keys National Marine Sanctuary.

Florida Keys National Marine Sanctuary Preservation Area, or SPA, as denoted by four large yellow marking buoys delineating the protected area. Accordingly, there is no harvesting here of fish or lobster or any live or dead matter.

Joy Williams reports in her sublimely written book, *The Florida Keys*, that another of the Coffins Patch reefs was once referred to as "Atlantis." She writes of towering pillar corals rising like great spires from the substrate as if to create the image of some magnificent though abstract underwater city.

However, much of this elegant décor was destroyed decades ago by hungry souvenir traders who toppled the spires, shipped them off, and sold them on retail shelves. Likely, Atlantis refers to what is today called Pillar Patch Reef.

Frankly, it was exactly that sort of destructive behavior that prompted John Pennekamp to fight for the sanctuary off the coast of Key Largo that would go on to bear his name. It is unfortunate that more men of his caliber have not fallen in love with the Florida Reef.

At a Glance

Name: Coffins Patch Reef
How to get there: This series of 6 distinct patch reefs found roughly 3.5 miles southeast of Key Colony Beach mostly sits in 10 to 30 feet of water. The Stake, the patch most commonly visited by the local charter trade, is designated a Species Preservation Area, so there is no fishing or harvesting within the boundaries of the four large yellow buoys. Coffins Patch reefs are easy to get to and are regularly visited by snorkeling charter outfits operating from Duck Key to the Seven Mile Bridge.

SNORKELING SITES

Reefs

R20 Reef   GPS: 24 40.500N/80 57.400W; Depth: 15–40 feet
Pillar Patch Reef   GPS: 24 40.950N/80 58.319W; Depth: 15 feet
The Stake   GPS: 24 41.100N/80 57.850W; Depth: 10–30 feet
Sand Circle Reef   GPS: 24 41.486N/80 56.581W; Depth: 15 feet
The Elbow   GPS: 24 41.540N/80 56.846W; Depth: 7–15 feet

Fun Facts

The San Pedro Underwater Archaeological State Preserve (GPS: 24 51.802N/80 40.795W) is located approximately 1.25 miles south of Indian Key. The *San Pedro* is another of the Spanish treasure fleet that was destroyed in the July hurricane of 1733. The 287-ton ship sank in 18 feet of water, though its remains—consisting of piles of ballast stones—were salvaged after its discovery in 1960. To celebrate the site, however, the state enhanced these ballast piles with seven replica cannons as well as a period anchor. Mooring buoys have been anchored to the substrate.

10

Sombrero Reef

Sombrero Reef is the primary snorkeling destination in the Middle Keys for three excellent reasons: shallow reefs, robust corals, and lots of fish. Simply put, there is a fiesta going on beneath the turquoise surface. Of course, the only way to account for both the mass of substrate and the intricate patterns of reef growth is time. A reef this structured can only be the result of thousands of years of coral polyp labor.

For the record, they have done an excellent job. Some of the local charter outfits claim that the reef is the top-rated destination in the Florida Keys. It is probably in the top 5. At the very least, the reef is a sight to see, as it is actually conceivable for a snorkeler to explore the nooks and crannies of this shallow reef site for hours without ever seeing the same patch of coral twice.

The reef is found 3.5 miles east of Marathon's Boot Key Harbor. It does not take a GPS system to locate the corals—they are marked by the tallest lighthouse punctuating the Florida Reef. Out at the light, just beneath the surface, sandy grooves mark the floor like white lines on an asphalt parking lot.

Sombrero is a spur-and-groove reef system. What those sandy grooves delineate are walls of limestone substrate that rise as much as 15 feet from the ocean floor like great spurs. It is carpeted with elegant sea fans, mounds of star corals, brain corals, fire corals, and sponges. Elkhorn corals, too, grow from the edges like great horned crowns.

As for the reef's name, its origin is unclear. Sometime between Juan Ponce de León's expedition of 1513 and the creation of George Gauld's 1774 chart, Spanish explorers named the locale Cayo Sombrero, a name that was later transformed to Sombrero Kay.

The site was referred to as Sombrero Kay rather than Sombrero Reef because, once upon a time, there was dry land here. J. W. Norie wrote of the islet, "About 5 miles S. 1/4 E. from the west end of Cayo Vaca, there is a small sandy kay on the reef, called by the Spaniards Cayo Sombrero; this is the easternmost kay on the reef" (Norie 20).

In John Lee Williams' early account of Florida, he calls the island Key Sombrero, describing it as "the easternmost islet on the reef. It is situated six or seven miles N.E. from Bahia Honda, and four miles S.W. from Knight's Key, the western key of the Vacas group. It is but a patch of rock, covered with a few mangroves and pieces of wreck" (J. L. Williams 41).

The site was also once referred to as Dry Bank. There seems to be no record of why "Sombrero" was associated with this former plot of land. Perhaps, from the point of view of a sailor, the way the little spit of sand appeared to sit atop a brim of coral heads gave the site the appearance of a big hat.

In any case, the obvious appearance of land, of an easternmost key, is probably why so few shipwrecks are associated with the reef. Even after the islet was blown asunder by some combination of time, tide, and hurricanes over a hundred years ago, wrecks still failed to pile up. The Coffins Patch reefs located nine miles to the north had been marked by a barrel mounted atop a 36-foot iron pole in 1852. This warning might have helped keep ships in deeper water, too.

Coffins Patch Reef was 1 of 15 reefs marked by James Totten and the Coastal Survey, and it was also the first site chosen for what would later become the Sombrero Key Lighthouse. Work on the 160-foot-high iron structure was still in the beginning stages at Coffins Patch Reef when a hurricane blew through on August 29, 1856, and destroyed the work platform.

After the storm, further construction plans were put on hold. It was decided that Sombrero Key would be a more stable location, and construction crews abandoned the Coffins Patch site to reconvene at Sombrero Key. Work began in 1857.

Sombrero Key Lighthouse was completed in 1858, and standing at 160 feet above the Atlantic seafloor, it is the tallest of the lights marking the Florida Reef. The focal point of the light is 142 feet above its base.

Like Carysfort Light built before it and Alligator Light built after, the Sombrero structure was placed atop a screw-pile octagonal base mounted on eight massive discs resting on the bottom. The iron beams supporting the structure were pounded into the limestone substrate by a steam-driven hammer to a depth of 10 feet, 1 inch at a time.

Also like Carysfort Light, Sombrero Light was constructed under the command of George G. Meade, a lieutenant in the Army Corps of Topographical Engineers. During the Civil War years, he would be promoted to general and command the Union Army of the Potomac. He would help defeat Robert E. Lee at the (second) battle of Gettysburg.

In fact, Sombrero Key Lighthouse was the last navigational beacon built to mark the Florida Reef before the Civil War. While the reef does not seem to have an extensive history of shipwrecks, one ship in particular did manage to leave an impression.

The *Louisiana* struck Sombrero Reef on October 17, 1910; it would take three months and repeated dynamite blasts to carve a path through the coral to dislodge it. Courtesy of Jerry Wilkinson Collection.

The double-masted French steamer SS *Louisiana* was driven onto the reef by hurricane-force winds and heavy waves on October 17, 1910. While all 600 passengers and crew were rescued by the U.S revenue cutter *Forward*, salvage of the ship itself proved a difficult and lengthy operation.

The Merritt and Chapman Derrick Wrecking Company eventually freed the vessel, though at some cost to the reef. Dynamite was used to free the *Louisiana*; unfortunately, such practices were common then. To dislodge the ship, the wreckers repeatedly blasted and removed chunks of destroyed coral reef until a small channel for the ship to egress was blown clear, a task that was not completed until February of 1911.

Looking at satellite images of Sombrero Reef today, there is definitely an anomaly out at the reef that stretches west from the lighthouse. It is either the trough left behind by the *Louisiana's* removal, or the deposit field from the land that once occupied Sombrero Key.

Like every lighthouse marking the reef, Sombrero Key Light was manned by a civilian crew until 1939, when all U.S. lighthouses were integrated into the U.S. Coast Guard under the Presidential Reorganization Act. In November of 1960, Boatswain Mate First Class Furman C. Williamson was assigned as officer-in-charge of Sombrero Key Lighthouse.

Like so many people, Williamson was afraid of the barracudas that apparently lurked beneath the iron structure even then. He explained to reporter John Watts in an article printed in the *Keynoter* newspaper on March 24, 1960, "There is no restriction against swimming, but we just don't dare take a chance."

When Hurricane Donna stormed across these middle keys in 1960, the four men on duty at the light were Chief Williamson, Engineman Ernest Bryan, Seaman Cecil Bryan, and Seaman Donald Beckman. The men reported 150-mile-per-hour gusts and 25-foot waves crashing against the lighthouse.

The bottom platform of the structure was ripped away by the wind and waves, but the living quarters, 40 feet above the water, remained a safe haven. A story appearing in the *Keynoter* on Thursday, October 27, 1960, reported one of the men as saying, "It was rough but we made it. We had plenty of steak and we had our own power generating plant."

The Sombrero Key Lighthouse remained a manned station until its automation in 1963. It can be seen by automobiles crossing the Seven Mile Bridge, and, like moths to a light, snorkelers should allow themselves to be drawn to the structure, as it indeed marks a fantastic snorkeling destination. What the reef has in its favor, what all Middle Keys reefs have in common, is that they are not growing offshore of Key West, Islamorada, or Key Largo, and as such have not suffered the same heavy traffic and degradation.

The verdant coral gardens growing here range from single-digit depths to around 35 feet. One of the most intriguing and unusual aspects of the reef is that it offers snorkelers an intimate view—because some of its corals grow so near the surface, snorkelers are afforded the chance to see the more intricate details of the reef so often obfuscated by depth. For instance, even for snorkelers uncomfortable with taking a big breath and diving down for a more intimate observation of the reef, it is possible to see colorful details such as tiny Christmas tree worms, which sprout like Dr. Seussian Douglas firs from the corals, or long-legged, candy-cane-like crustaceans called banded coral shrimp that step lightly over the reef.

At a Glance

Name: Sombrero Reef

How to get there: This massive spur-and-groove coral reef formation growing in 5 to 35 feet of water is marked by the Sombrero Key Lighthouse, the tallest of the markers built along the Florida Reef. Sombrero Reef might be one of the easiest sites for snorkelers to visit through local charters, as the reef is the main draw of the Middle Keys. Finding a charter boat heading out to the reef on any given day is as hard as pulling off the Overseas Highway. Basically every snorkeling charter in the Marathon area visits Sombrero.

SNORKELING SITES

Reefs

Sombrero Reef   GPS: 24 37.520N/81 06.730W; Depth: 5–35 feet

Fun Facts

For snorkelers willing to float and watch the sometimes intricate interplay between species on a reef, there exists an opportunity to witness firsthand what biologists refer to as a cleaning station.

While every reef has them, shallow Sombrero Reef provides easy viewing for those who are patient. These cleaning stations operate like any drive-thru—or, in this case, swim-thru—personal detailing service. For instance, a barracuda will swim up to a specific coral head or ledge much the same way a car pulls into a car wash. The fish is serviced by a cadre of wrasses, gobies, and delicate shrimp like the exquisitely blue-shaded Pederson's cleaning shrimp.

Their job is to scour the barracuda clean of parasites—from its body, inside the gills, and between the barracuda's wicked teeth. When the shrimp, gobies, and wrasses have done their job, the barracuda swims away; then perhaps a black grouper pulls up, and all the little cleaners go back to work.

It is not always barracuda and grouper pulling in, however—snappers, grunts, angelfish, even turtles and eels swim through. Sometimes the waiting line can be two or three fish long. And yes, while this is generally a relationship of trust and mutually beneficial, every once in a while the barracuda or grouper snacks on one of the gobies or wrasses. But, to be fair, every once in a while the cleaner fish will take a small fleshy bite out of its client, too.

11

Bahia Honda State Park

Beachcombers come for the naturally occurring sand beaches, a rare commodity on this craggy limestone archipelago. Campers come to walk the beach, snorkel, fish, and toast marshmallows over an open fire before sandwiching the squishy-melty-goo between a piece of chocolate and a graham cracker. As for the snorkelers, they come for the fruitful shallows a coconut's throw from the beach.

Snorkelers will not find the elaborate, stunning reef structures built from hundreds and thousands of years of coral polyp labor this close to shore. Instead, they will swim over a substrate covered with crevices and rock piles, old lobster traps, sponges, and small, sometimes diminutive, offerings of both soft and hard corals.

The trick to successfully snorkeling these inshore sites, referred to as hard-bottom coral communities, is to go slowly. Of course, this can be said for every snorkeling adventure. The first one to finish does not win a prize. Rather, investigate anything that rises from the semi-sandy Atlantic seafloor—the craggier the better—as the underwater world tends to congregate around these structures.

As you float, look for the long red antenna of spiny lobsters sticking out from under a sponge or a low-profile coral head. Purple sea urchins will inhabit the nooks and crannies of the substrate like spiny blueberry filling. Do not reach down and touch them, however, as they are mildly venomous.

Yellow-and-purple damselfish will be fearlessly guarding their territory, their little piece of the reef, against all intruders, be they snappers, wrasses, or juvenile surgeonfish no bigger than fifty-cent pieces.

Additionally, and it is illustrative of the argument that the queen conch population is making a comeback after the conches were commercially overharvested in the 1970s and 1980s, it is common to see these massive sea snails patrolling the bottom here. Of course, Bahia Honda has been a popular destination for more than conchs for hundreds of years.

This is not only because of the island's naturally occurring sand beaches, but also because of its *bahia honda*, or deep bay. After the aboriginals, sailors were the first drawn to the still bay of the crescent harbor. At 30 feet, it is one of the deepest natural harbors in the whole of the Florida Keys. While the obvious identifier has stuck through the years, the island has known other names. Bahia Honda, however, in one form or another, has prevailed.

One of the earliest variations was penned by Father Alana when he named it *Baia Onda* on his 1743 chart. Another Spaniard, Juan Elixio de la Puente, called the island Cayo de Bayahonda on his 1765 chart. The first surveyor general for British East Florida, William Gerard de Brahn, took another approach and called the key Rice Island on his 1772 chart. There is no obvious reason for that name.

George Gauld, a Scottish-born surveyor sent to map Florida's difficult waters, wrote of the island: "The Harbour of Bahia Honda may easily be known by the tall palmetto cabbage-trees of the Long Island on the right hand coming in; they make it the more

Bahia Honda State Park boasts some of the most beautiful beaches in the Keys, and in 1992 one was declared the Best Beach in America. Photo by Brad Bertelli.

remarkable, as there are no cabbage-trees to the westward of it, on any of the Kays that are on the Reef" (13).

He also remarked that, "Bahia Honda, like Cayo Hueso, is much frequented by the Turtlers and Wreckers from Providence and by the Spanish vessels from Havana, of which there are about 10 annually employed in fishing among the Kays on the coast of Florida, where there is sufficient quantity of fish to supply the West Indies" (13).

In a book of sailing directions written by J. W. Norie and published in 1860, the key was referred to as "a mile long, with a sandy beach, remarkable for a number of tall palmetto cabbage-trees, the first of the kind you fall in with coming from the westward; this island is therefore called Cabbage Tree Island" (19).

This statement is misleading because he was not really calling the island of Bahia Honda Cabbage Tree Island. Like Gauld before him, Norie described Bahia Honda as a collection of three islands, with Cabbage Tree being only one. What also made Bahia Honda such a popular locale was that, as Gauld said, it was a source for "very good fresh water" (17).

John Lee Williams suggested that a small settlement existed on the east end of the island during the 1820s and 1830s. "There is a small, but pleasant settlement on the east side of the harbor, with a well of good water" (37).

He also indicates that Bahia Honda was then considered a collection of multiple islands. "Cabbage Island is the longest of a considerable cluster of islets, called the Honda Keys. It is two miles long, and two-thirds of a mile wide; it is covered with tall cabbage trees interspersed with fruits and flowers, and appears rich and pleasant, but we did not explore the interior of the island" (37).

In any case, the name ambiguity would be settled once and for all by F. H. Gerdes, who wrote, "The large island called on the chart Cabbage Tree Island is the Bahia Honda Key" (46). It has been Bahia Honda ever since. Gerdes also indicates in his work that the island's freshwater supply was turned brackish by an 1846 hurricane.

With the turn of the century, big changes were in store for Bahia Honda. The island was mapped and charted by Henry Flagler's surveyors and, by 1908, construction of the Oversea Railway had reached the island, where workers were living in two-story dormitories. The work was hard, the heat oppressive, and the marauding hordes of mosquitoes thirsty. Also, there was the matter of bridging the deep bay.

Having completed the Seven Mile Bridge, railroad workers must have looked at the 5,055 feet separating Bahia Honda Key from Spanish Harbor Key as a drop in the bucket, a piece of cake, a narrow expanse. To the contrary, of the 43 bridges needed to link mainland Florida to Key West, the Bahia Honda Bridge proved one of the most difficult to construct. This was due, in no small part, to the dangerously strong currents created in the pass by the deep harbor.

For safety reasons, workdays were cut to two 45-minute shifts during slack tide, the short time between high and low tides when the water becomes still. Additionally, because of the channel's depth, the necessary support beams required a great deal of material. A single piling in the center of the structure required an entire boatload of sand, gravel, and cement to construct. In fact, when a hurricane that blew across Bahia Honda in 1910 raged for 30 hours, it managed to displace part of the bridge foundation, and another shipload of materials was required to repair it.

It was January 22, 1912, when the Key West Extension officially opened and the railroad delivered Henry Flagler, an octogenarian at the time, from the mainland to Key West. During the course of its operation, the Key West Extension of the Florida East Coast Railway made regular stops on Bahia Honda. Passengers would disembark to picnic and swim in the warm, clear waters.

Back on board, when the train would pass through the camel-back bridge, passengers were told to keep their hands and heads inside the train as it rambled and roared 25 feet above the turquoise waters. Unfortunately, the Oversea Railway was a relatively short-lived venture, as it was ultimately destroyed on Monday, September 2, 1935.

It was Labor Day. A Category 5 hurricane ripped across the Upper Keys and destroyed communities on the Matecumbes, Windley Key, and in Tavernier. Among other casualties, the train sent from the mainland on a rescue mission was toppled like so many cardboard boxes. The train was pushed off its tracks on Upper Matecumbe Key, near what is today the Islamorada Post Office.

Two-hundred-mile-per-hour winds and 17-foot storm surges destroyed nearly everything they came up against, including this rescue train sent from the mainland. Courtesy of Jerry Wilkinson Collection.

Up to 200-mile-per-hour winds and 17-foot storm surges assailed the island. The cars were pushed over and the tracks treated like tiddlywinks. Only the locomotive engine, number 447, withstood the blow.

Ultimately, when it came time to repair the train tracks, the owners decided to go in a different direction. Eventually, the Oversea Railway was covered up with asphalt and cement and converted into the Oversea Highway. Private companies were contracted out to transform the bridges from rail to road.

The Cleary Brothers were chosen for the Bahia Honda Bridge conversion job. Because of the bridge's narrow aperture, they decided to go over its top, not through it. A concrete slab was poured over the reinforced trusses at the top of the camelback bridge. When cars subsequently drove over the bridge, they were 65 feet above the fast-moving turquoise waters of the *bahia honda*.

The Oversea Highway opened to traffic on March 29, 1938. Originally, it was a toll road run by the Oversea Road and Toll Bridge District, which also maintained part of Bahia Honda as a public park. Like the train before them, passenger cars stopped and people picnicked and frolicked at one of the covered tables along the key's crescent beach.

By 1950, the park had a gas station (near where the marina parking lot lies today) and a concession stand with cold drinks and hot dogs. Still, there was no electricity on the island, and everything ran with the aid of loudly humming generators. There was, however, another side to the island—the residents of Marathon had been instructed by the county to use the northern end of the island as a dump.

Not until the late 1950s and early 1960s did the park that Bahia Honda is now world famous for begin to evolve. Between 1953 and 1957, the land was signed over to Monroe County, and by 1961, the county had budgeted $8,000 for a park caretaker and a cleanup team.

By September of 1961, Bahia Honda had been turned over to the Florida Board of Parks and Historic Memorials. Alva Cook became the park's first superintendent. She hired two rangers: James R. Smith and Johnny Johnston in May of 1962. Sadly, it was not until 1963 that Monroe County officials declared the dumping of trash on Bahia Honda unlawful. It can be assumed that, for some residents, old habits died hard.

Still, improvements were being made. On July 15, 1966, electricity was delivered and the constant, ungentle hum of the generators used to run the gas station and concession stand ceased.

Over the ensuing years, Bahia Honda has grown into one conch pearl of a Florida state park. In April of 1966, 91.7 acres were acquired for state park land, with another 190 placed on the books for purchase the following year. The iconic Bahia Honda Bridge closed to all traffic in 1972 when an earlier version of the current bridge system opened.

The island still stands out for its natural sand beaches and people still stop, every day, to picnic and splash in the warm, shallow waters. The park's main draw is its beaches, and it advertises three. Two spill gently into the turquoise hues of the Atlantic and one into the Gulf of Mexico.

On the Gulf of Mexico side, concrete-covered picnic enclaves cast shadows across the sand while the broken camelback bridge looms in the background. Of the two Atlantic beaches, Sandspur Beach is clearly the more striking. The melding of white sand and gently ebbing and flowing tide creates a breathtaking landscape. The beach is a brilliant locale for sunbathing and swimming.

The best snorkeling beach is Loggerhead Beach, which can appear as barely more than a narrow expanse of sand, especially at high tide. Sometimes there is not enough room to spread out a towel without fear of it getting wet. The activity in the shallows, however, is nothing short of magical. Wade out to the sandbar before donning your gear and then swim slowly over the seagrass beds.

It would be a mistake to kick furiously and overlook these emerald fields. They can be home to starfish, whelks, and conchs, including horse conchs—the Florida state shell—and the pink or queen conch, the symbol of this archipelago. On occasion, the horse conch can be seen extending its massive orange foot and devouring a queen conch—it is an awesome sight.

After the seagrass beds, you will spot a small forest of soft corals called slimy sea feathers that grow out of the limestone substrate like purple ostrich plumes. Occasionally, a magnificently colored snail called the flamingo tongue can be seen sliding slowly over one of the delicate coral branches. Based solely on coloration, the snail should be called an orange-dotted giraffe tongue, but that is another story.

Bahia Honda is a must-see snorkeling adventure. For snorkeling without the benefit of offshore transportation, Bahia Honda is the best beach in the chain. Snorkeling gear, including dive flags (required by state law), can be rented at the park.

The big downside to snorkeling here is that, on windy days, when the surface is choppy, the visibility suffers. If whitecaps are visible from the beach, it probably is not the best day to snorkel. This will prove a tragedy for those passers-through with only one day allotted for the experience.

When conditions are right, however, the magical world underneath this turquoise blanket is crystal clear.

At a Glance

Name: Bahia Honda State Park
Location: 36850 Overseas Highway, Bahia Honda Key
Web site: www.floridastateparks.org/bahiahonda

How to get there: This park is a hop, skip, and a jump from the southernmost end of the Seven Mile Bridge. Because it is a state park, there is a nominal entrance fee. Plan to arrive early on holiday weekends as the park can, and probably will, fill to capacity. For the best snorkeling, pull into the park, pay the fee at the ranger shack, and proceed. Drive until the fork in the road and then turn right. If possible, park in the small lot on the left-hand side. If not, park in the marina parking lot and walk back across the road to Loggerhead Beach. Perfect for the whole family, this hard-bottom coral community is an ideal locale, with depths ranging from 1 to 5 feet.

SNORKELING SITES

Loggerhead Beach

Fun Facts

Sandspur Beach is an award-winning beach singled out as the best beach in America by both *Condé Nast Traveler* and Dr. Beach himself (Stephen Leatherman). Since 1991, Dr. Beach has announced the best beach in America like an Academy Award.

Remarkably, both opinions were rendered in the same year, 1992. What makes for an award-winning beach? According to Dr. Beach, factors such as the size of breaking waves, water temperature, softness of sand, number of sunny days annually, smell, public safety, accessibility, and vistas are but a handful of the 50 criteria considered.

While Sandspur Beach is a onetime reigning champion, it is not the best snorkeling beach the park has to offer. That title goes to Loggerhead Beach, found at the southern end of the island; park in the small lot across from the marina.

12

Looe Key

Approximately 6 miles off Big Pine Key, Looe Key is thriving. This massive spur-and-groove reef formation, one of the most developed snorkeling reefs in the chain, is a brilliant spectacle. Armies of blue tangs swim elegantly over the coral beds as flocks of midnight parrotfish as big as basset hounds peck at the corals. Underwater, the chomping sound of their feeding is akin to celery being chewed.

After the briefest of snorkels, it quickly becomes absolutely clear that, between the robust shapes and brilliant colors, there is a great deal going on at this particular reef. Suffice it to say that Looe Key is one of the Florida Reef's top 5 snorkels. Rest assured that octopi are slinking about this coral garden.

One of the shallowest reefs in the chain, Looe Key's corals grow so near the surface that when the Atlantic rolls over some of the shallower beds, a white froth whips up atop the turquoise water like a meringue. As such, even casual snorkelers who prefer to stay at the surface are able to witness firsthand some of the more intricate details hiding in the reef's nooks and crannies: banded shrimp, Christmas tree worms, and the sometimes neon details of tiny fish called gobies.

The name Looe Key might sound a little bit confusing as this is a reef site. Once upon a time, there was a narrow stretch of dry land here, but this particular islet was swept back into the Atlantic by a hurricane well over a hundred years ago.

In any case, the site is named after the HMS *Looe*, the fourth of six British ships of war given that particular name between 1696 and 1763. The *Looe* that ended her career on the Florida Reef was constructed at the shipyard of Snelgrove in Limehouse, an area of London. It was launched on the River Thames on December 12, 1741. The ship was 124 feet in length and had a beam of 36 feet. The *Looe* was armed with 44 guns.

Back when the territories of South Carolina and Georgia were under British control, La Florida belonged to Spain. Because Spanish privateers had ventured into the Georgia territory to attack on at least one occasion, a fleet of Royal Navy ships headed by Captain Utting and the HMS *Looe* was sent to Charleston, South Carolina, to help protect the coastline and the Florida Straits.

It was February 2, 1744, when Captain Utting came upon a suspicious-looking ship flying a French flag near Cuba. When the *Looe* approached, a large oilskin packet was observed being thrown overboard, which the crew of the *Looe* was quick to retrieve. When Captain Utting read the papers, he discovered that, while the vessel was indeed flying French flags, it was the captured English merchant vessel *Billander Betty*. Furthermore, the ship was being used by the Spanish!

Captain Utting took control of the vessel and placed a crew aboard to marshal the *Betty*. The two ships then began sailing back to Charleston. On the second night of the trip, the HMS *Looe* sailed past Cayo Hueso, an early moniker of Key West. Every half hour thereafter, the crew dropped a sounding lead to measure the water depth. Around midnight on February 4, satisfied with the safety of the ship, Captain Utting went belowdecks to his cabin. Approximately one hour later, everything changed. The men on watch suddenly saw waves breaking over a shallow reef system. An alarm was sounded and evasive actions were taken. The *Looe's* rudder struck the reef and broke off, and the ship, unable to steer, was pounded by swells and beaten against the coral beds. It was sinking fast. To make matters worse, a few minutes later, the *Billander Betty* struck the reef too.

The sailors managed to escape to the small key that used to exist on the reef. Fortunately, no lives were lost. When the sun emerged over the Atlantic's horizon, a mixture of emotions must have been percolating among the 274 survivors crowding the thin layer of sand rising about a foot out of the clear turquoise waters. According to Captain Utting's written account, the islet was approximately 300 yards long and 100 yards wide.

The dilemma for the survivors was threefold. Not only was this Spanish territory, but Tequesta Indians inhabited the archipelago and, unfortunately for those men standing on the barren key, the Keys' natives made a sporadic living off of these shipwrecks.

These Indians were prone to killing survivors. Spanish sailors were the exception, and were often held captive because they could be ransomed. Another aspect of their current predicament, however, was that a storm could roll through and wash them off the key.

All was not lost, however, as the survivors had managed to salvage the ship's boats, 20 bags of bread, and 6 barrels of gunpowder. There was even a glimmer of hope when a Spanish sloop passed by the wreck site. After spying the English, however, it quickly sailed off. Captain Utting ordered three boats manned with armed marines to capture the ship at all costs.

No one came back that night, but the following day the sloop sailed up with the three boats in tow. It became clear that, in the end, with the help of the captured Spanish sloop, every man stranded on the islet would sail away to safety.

While nothing is left of the *Looe* but its memory and some piles of ballast stones, Looe Key remains a snorkeling gold mine. The reef formations grow in 5 to 25 feet of water, but care should be taken when snorkeling too close to the shallowest coral beds, as the ebb and flow of the tide can prove dangerous. For snorkeler safety, as well as that of the corals, snorkeling over a reef in less than 2 feet of water is not recommended.

Another interesting tidbit about Looe Key is that it is an excellent place to see a shark. The dark blue line in the water visible from the reef is the demarcation between the blue of the Atlantic and that deeper shade of the Gulf Stream. It is the Gulf Stream that is responsible for the frequent shark sightings out at the reef.

Do not be afraid of the sharks. Instead, marvel at the liquid way they cruise through the water. In fact, should a lucky snorkeler happen upon one of these big, elegant fish swimming at the reef, the glimpse will likely prove a fleeting one. Truth be told, sharks consider snorkelers little more than something to get away from.

Three species of sharks are specifically sighted at Looe Key: nurse sharks, Caribbean reef sharks, and black tips. None of these fish should be deemed a threat. Should a shark present itself, it is unnecessary to begin shaking in one's flippers. Instead, feel good about the fish tale in the making.

There should honestly be more sharks out at the reef, but as it is, sightings are hit-and-miss. There are a number of reasons. Largely, it is because they have been hunted like rats, shot at, gillnetted, and overfished.

Peter Benchley bears at least some of the blame. It is unfortunate, but his novel spawned some of the most dangerous fiction ever written, at least for sharks. It was perhaps still more unfortunate that the book led to a blockbuster movie starring Roy Scheider and Richard Dreyfuss.

Benchley's seminal tale pricked a fearful nerve in the collective consciousness and demonized sharks as a whole. Believe it or not, after audiences first watched *Jaws* in 1975, some people were not only afraid of the beach, but of their swimming pools, bathtubs, and even showers. As a result, the big fish were considered cold-blooded killers, and the association stuck to them like a bloody resin.

To put the whole shark scare into perspective, statistically speaking it is a far more dangerous proposition to drive a car—for any distance—than to snorkel in Florida waters. In fact, snorkelers are much more likely to be mauled by a dog, swarmed by bees, or win the lottery than have a negative encounter with a shark.

Instead of worrying about sharks, snorkelers would be much better off making sure they have applied a suitable sunscreen to their exposed flesh. While shark attacks are rare events in the Florida Keys, horrible sunburns are not.

In any case, full disclosure dictates the unveiling of the true bully of the coral reef, the damselfish. As a family, damselfish present the classic Napoleon complex. These one-to–five-inch fish are fearless and will defend their little patches of the reef against all comers. Place a finger into the territory of a damselfish, leave it there like an intrusion, and the affront will surely be rebuffed.

At a Glance

Name: Looe Key

How to get there: Looe Key is another easily accessible reef found approximately 6 miles off the coast of Big Pine Key. Charter boats in operation from Bahia Honda to Ramrod Key visit the reef twice daily, weather permitting. A shallow spur-and-groove reef formation growing in 5 to 35 feet of water, this area is probably the most frequently visited snorkeling site in the Lower Keys.

SNORKELING SITES

Reefs

Looe Key   GPS: 24 32.700N/81 24.500W; Depths: 5–35 feet

Fun Facts

For the last quarter of a century, this reef has been home to the Looe Key Underwater Music Festival. The event is held on the first Saturday after the Fourth of July.

It is a delightfully offbeat festival where scuba divers and snorkelers are afforded the opportunity to explore a beautiful tract of coral reef while listening to Jimmy Buffett tunes broadcast

It never ceases to thrill when a turtle cruises by a reef, especially one as spectacular as Looe Key. Photo by Krissy Gustinger.

through a series of strategically placed underwater Lubell System speakers.

The event was first conceived in 1985 by Bill Becker, former disc jockey and current news director at U.S. 1 Radio, 104.1 FM, and Dr. Fred Troxel, a dentist from Big Pine Key. Becker has been maintaining the integrity of the playlist ever since.

In addition to Jimmy Buffett and mainstays like the Beatles' *Octopus's Garden*, Becker plays reggae tunes and the recorded songs of humpback whales. "I like percussion," Becker says. "Percussion makes a good sound underwater. And new age music, we play some of that. And it's all commercial free. For four hours, from ten until two."

The festival is an effort to educate as well as entertain. Coral reefs are important biological and ecological systems, not merely for the benefit of divers, snorkelers, and the tourism industry. As such, in addition to the four hours of commercial-free music, recorded public service announcements from the Florida Keys National Marine Sanctuary promoting diver etiquette and coral reef awareness are broadcast. The event is simulcast live on the radio and streamed over the Internet worldwide from U.S. 1 Radio, 104.1 FM.

The annual event is sponsored by the Lower Keys Chamber of Commerce and the Florida Keys Council of the Arts. Those interested in participating should contact the Lower Keys Chamber of Commerce (www.lowerkeyschamber.com) for all the latest details. And, for the record, if there really was such a thing as an octopus's garden, Looe Key would totally have one.

13

Key West Marine Park

The coral reefs offshore of Key West can provide some excellent snorkeling fare. In fact, the barkers standing along Duval Street expend a fair amount of energy extolling them. "Come," they call out from their kiosks, "explore the only living barrier reef in North America. The third largest of its kind in the world! Swim eye-to-eye with an angelfish."

While there is truth to their spiels and every attempt should be made to explore the reefs offshore, there is a little-known snorkeling opportunity much closer to Duval Street—the Key West Marine Park.

The park waters are located on the south side of the island and stretch nearly all the way from the end of Duval Street (not the Mallory Square end) to the White Street Pier. There are four public access points to the park: three from beaches and one from Mary and John Spottswood Park at the foot of Seminole Street. Beach access points include South Beach at the southern end of Duval Street, Dog Beach at the end of Vernon Street, and Higgs Beach at the end of White Street. Those staying at either the Casa Marina

Whenever snorkeling, and especially at shallow sites like the Marine Park, it is important to keep an eye out for gems like sea anemones. Photo by Krissy Gustinger.

or the Reach resorts have access to the park right from the beach of their respective resort.

It is important to remember that this park is here for everyone to enjoy—please do not take the lobster should a pair of spiny red antennae be sticking out from some crevice. The park is a voluntary no-take zone.

The designated swim areas are indicated by a series of demarcation buoys 600 feet from shore. In terms of snorkeling, note that while each access point is an excellent spot to cool off, some parts of the park make for better snorkeling than others. One spot in particular makes for the best snorkeling of all.

This is off Higgs Beach, specifically near the end of Reynolds Street, as this locale has significantly more structure than any other section of the park.

The big coral heads found at the reefs have not been established here. Rather, these shallows offer a more subtle experience. Interested snorkelers willing to explore the park will be rewarded by its surprising biodiversity.

There is a great deal to see. Granted, the vast majority of the park is carpeted by beds of seagrass, and seagrass is not the most vibrant environment. Remember that it can prove surprising, though, as small vase and barrel sponges can be found here, as well as spiny lobster and conch. Conchs are commonly sighted in the park. Sometimes they are pink-lipped queen conchs and sometimes they are other varieties, like milk or horse conchs, as all manner of gastropods frequent the area. The seagrass beds can also harbor starfish.

While a few fish can be spotted out over the open seagrass beds, they are not generally considered a big tropical fish draw. Rest assured, there are tropical fish close by. To find them, snorkel out to the remnants of the old pier sticking out of the water like broken kneecaps near the end of Reynolds Street.

The pilings are generally adorned by pelicans, seagulls, or cormorants. Even considering the aviary accoutrements, at first glance these surroundings might appear relatively uneventful to the unsuspecting snorkeler. Just below the surface, however, life is bustling.

In a manner of speaking, the pieces of the old pier that have collapsed into the water have become a sort of artificial reef. The corrugated metal acts as a fair substitute for the limestone substrate of an actual reef wall because, just like a natural reef, its surface

The hogfish, pictured here, is a succulent local favorite. Hogfish frequent both near-shore sites like the Key West Marine Park and offshore reefs. Courtesy of Bill Brecht, Florida Keys National Marine Sanctuary.

is slowly becoming encrusted with colorful bouquets of algae and sponges. Corals, too, have melded to the surface like pottery.

A great many colorful reef fish are attracted to this old pier. While it is impossible to foretell conditions or a species count on any given day, schools of the ubiquitous snappers, chubs, and grunts swarm around the old pier posts on a daily basis.

A surprising number of fish more closely associated with coral reefs also frequent the area. A diligent observer could likely tally 50 individual species on any given snorkeling adventure. The list would include an array of damselfish, some of which are strikingly scaled in yellow and royal blue, as well as wrasses, parrotfish, butterflyfish, barracuda, and juvenile blue tangs the size of quarters. Ironically, at this stage of their development, the disc-shaped blue tangs are actually a canary yellow.

This park exists thanks to Reef Relief, founded by Craig and Deevon Quirolo, who moved to the Lower Keys in the 1970s. They were enamored with the turquoise waters and decided to educate boaters, divers, snorkelers, and anyone else who would listen about the fragility of the Florida Reef.

As a result, Reef Relief was born in 1987. One of the first objectives of the organization was to make boaters aware of the damage being done to corals by captains haphazardly tossing their anchors overboard. Reef Relief commissioned a project to install a system of 116 mooring buoys around 7 Key West coral reefs. The recipients of those buoys were Western Dry Docks, Sand Key, Rock Key, Eastern Docks, Western Sambo, Pelican Shoal, and Cottrell Key. Now, instead of dropping anchor, boats are able to safely tie off to a mooring buoy.

The Key West Marine Park is another of Reef Relief's projects. It is the island's only underwater park, and is essentially an area designated as a safe haven for swimmers and snorkelers to enjoy the water without the threat of boats or errant WaveRunners mindlessly speeding around.

The original premise of the park was threefold. The first goal was to create a place where swimmers and snorkelers could safely enjoy the waters. The second was to promote public awareness of near-shore water quality. The third never happened.

Reef Relief wanted to create an inshore coral reef nursery, but it never came to fruition. This was due in part to political red tape and partly because the site was too shallow and vulnerable to storms and other inshore hazards like swimmers and snorkelers.

When the park was first developed in 2001, Michael Proimosm, representing Wyndam International's Casa Marina Resort and Beach House, as well as the Reach Resort, donated $40,000. These resorts are Waldorf Astoria properties now.

The project was also selected by the Coastal Partnership Program of the Florida Department of Community Affairs for funding during the grant cycle of July 2001 through June 2002. The $25,000 award was used by Reef Relief to install 33 demarcation buoys indicating three swimming lanes and two vessel access lanes. The money was also used to produce brochures promoting the underwater park.

At a Glance

Name: Key West Marine Park
How to get there: This is one of the few snorkeling sites that can be driven, bicycled, or walked to. The best snorkeling opportunity can be accessed right from Higgs Beach. Higgs Beach is found between White and Reynolds streets, and the remnants of the old dock offer the best show.

The Key West Marine Park brochure can be found at Reef Relief's Key West headquarters and environmental center at Schooner Wharf, next door to Conch Republic Seafood, at 631 Greene Street. It can also be found online at www.reefrelief.org/pdf/kwmpbrch.pdf.

SNORKELING SITES

Higgs Beach

Fun Facts

In 1982, a serpent wearing mirrored sunglasses slithered across the lone stretch of asphalt linking mainland North America to its most famous archipelago, the Florida Keys. Thick as a squad car, the beast situated itself across the highway and blocked traffic along U.S. 1, the only land-based conduit into and out of the Keys. The nightmare unfolded on Sunday, April 18, just after three o'clock in the afternoon. The scene of the crime was right in front of Skeeter Dyer's Last Chance Saloon, found at the southernmost extreme of Florida City.

The head of the beast was a cadre of federal agents directing Florida Highway Patrol officers and Border Patrol agents to install the flashing red lights and barricades of a U.S. border checkpoint. In the eyes of everyone living in the Keys, the act was an egregious display. While the checkpoint lasted only for a couple of weeks, it managed to change the identity of the islands forever.

The result was that all northbound traffic came to an immediate and painful halt. Armed men approached each vehicle, asking not only for identification, but for proof of citizenship—and not just from the drivers! Leaving the Florida Keys had become tantamount to leaving Canada or Mexico.

It did not take long for the resulting traffic snarl to stretch all the way to Key Largo, 18 miles away. The 20- or 25-minute drive from Key Largo to Florida City was now taking hours—3, 4, and sometimes 10—with no place to stop along the 18-mile stretch for a bite to eat or a drink or even to use the bathroom.

International media billed the quagmire as the world's biggest parking lot. To the detriment of those who inhabited the islands and made their living largely off of tourist dollars, the negative message being delivered was that, while the Florida Keys might be America's backyard paradise and vacationers were encouraged to drive down and visit, it was going to be absolute hell getting out.

The roadblock devastated the region's economy. Hotel rooms emptied; grouper and Key West pink shrimp began to spoil in the coolers of waterfront restaurants. Barstools gathered a fine layer of dust. The roadblock was choking the life out of the tourist industry and, as local wallets emptied and bank accounts began to drain, normally laid-back hackles began to rise.

Key West's mayor at the time, Dennis Wardlow, filed an injunction in Miami Superior Court, hoping to have the checkpoint lifted. The case was heard by Chief Federal Judge Clyde Atkins of the U.S. District Court. Just after 2 p.m. on Thursday, April 22, Wardlow and his constituents were told that, while the checkpoint would not be dismantled, it would cease to operate in its previous, egregious manner.

Mayor Wardlow left the courthouse with his head held high. He stopped on the courthouse steps to make a statement to a smattering of reporters that would change everything. Wardlow, along with a handful of stalwarts from the Key West community, decided that if the U.S. government was going to treat the Florida Keys as a foreign destination, then that is exactly what the islands would become. Wardlow announced that the Florida Keys would be seceding from the United States of America at noon the following day.

Mayor Wardlow and his advisors gathered at Clinton Square and declared the Keys the Conch Republic. A uniformed Navy officer in attendance was pummeled in the head with a loaf of Cuban bread (he had been forewarned of the event). Seconds later, the Conch Republic surrendered. As a fallen nation, though not a crestfallen people, Prime Minister Wardlow applied for $1 billion in foreign aid and war relief. Those funds were never received, but ever since that day, three flags have flown over the Florida Keys: the American flag, the Florida state flag, and the conch-emblazoned flag of the Conch Republic.

Because island denizens need little or no excuse to throw a party, it was decided that an annual independence celebration would be held every April thereafter. The occasion was declared Conch Republic Days.

Unfortunately, by the eighth anniversary of the event, the celebration was about to be shelved by the Key West Association for Tourist Development. Peter Anderson, along with Paul and Evalena Worthington, who own iconic Key West hangout Schooner Wharf Bar, reconfigured the failing Conch Republic Days into the wildly more successful 10-day-long Conch Republic Independence Celebration.

For Anderson's extensive efforts, then-Key-West-mayor and acting prime minister Tony Tarracino, the infamous Captain Tony of Captain Tony's Saloon, appointed Anderson the royal position of secretary general of the Conch Republic.

Peter Anderson currently serves as president of the board of directors at Reef Relief, a global nonprofit membership organization dedicated to protecting coral reefs.

14

Dry Tortugas National Park

The Dry Tortugas represent the best beach snorkel the Florida Keys—in fact, the whole of the Sunshine State—have to offer. The site's only real fault is its geographical inconvenience. Considered the end of the archipelago, the Dry Tortugas are located some 70 miles southwest of Key West.

The primary destination for the charter trade is Garden Key's Fort Jefferson. The uncompleted Civil War–era brick behemoth was built to protect the shipping lanes. Today, a visit to the fort is a wonderfully escapist excursion—one of the best Key West has to offer.

Once upon a time, water this clear and an environment this robust were common fare up and down the Florida Keys. The charter boat will dock at Garden Key. Snorkelers will be able to access the water from either South Swim Beach or North Swim Beach.

Snorkelers will also want to explore the outer wall of the moat. Over scores of years, the brick and mortar have proved a source of structure for coral polyps and sponges to populate. There are larger coral heads in the deeper waters close to the buoys marking

This aerial photograph of Garden Key, the most popular snorkeling destination in the Dry Tortugas, shows just how impressive Civil War–era Fort Jefferson still is. Courtesy of the National Parks Service.

the end of the designated snorkeling area. Look for any source of structure, as life will revolve around it. Be sure, too, to investigate the old wood pilings sticking up from the water on the eastern side of the fort, for they can likewise prove to be a haven where marine life congregates.

The intrepid explorer Juan Ponce de León first recorded this fringe of the Florida archipelago. He sailed into its midst with the small fleet of vessels supporting his New World expedition of 1513.

It was a June day, and the shallows beneath the wooden hulls of his ships must have shimmered with schools of ruddy snappers and yellow-and-blue-striped grunts.

The cries and calls of tens—maybe hundreds—of thousands of egrets, terns, boobies, and gulls roosting on the islands would have echoed loudly against the surface of the water. Caribbean monk seals, too, would have been seen sunning on the soft sand beaches, perhaps barking at the Spanish interlopers the way pinnipeds tend to do.

What Ponce de León also saw, however, besides the birds and seals, were turtles. There were so many turtles, in fact, that when Ponce de León placed his pen to the chart he was drawing, he formally named this intimate collection of islands Las Tortugas, the Turtles.

In their natural environment, the loggerhead, hawksbill, and green turtles that were once so prevalent in these waters move like quicksilver. It was fortunate for the sailors that they arrived in June, when, during the early summer months, pregnant turtles laboriously crawl onto tropical and subtropical beaches to bury their eggs in sandy nests. Exposed on dry land, turtles prove cumbersome creatures, and for the sailors who came ashore to fortify their rations with fresh meat, easy pickings.

Sailors simply walked up to the hapless reptiles and flipped them over onto their backs. It took some effort, as the turtles can weigh anywhere from 200 to 500 pounds, but overnight, Ponce de León's men reportedly captured 160 turtles as well as "fourteen seals . . . many pelicans and other birds that amounted to five thousand" (Dean 74).

Sadly, this would prove the beginning of the end for the Caribbean monk seal. The seals, a rich source of protein, were easily hunted by hungry sailors, for they were reportedly readily approachable by man. Now extinct, the last official Caribbean monk seal sighting was reported in 1952.

This Holder sketch, published in *Harper's New Monthly Magazine*, shows the technique used when capturing turtles on the beach. Courtesy of Jerry Wilkinson Collection.

Turtles, however, were the jackpot. Turtle meat was especially valuable because it could be kept fresh. Before modern refrigeration, the best way to keep meat fresh was to keep it alive. And turtles could be kept alive for days, flipped on their backs down in the dark of a ship's hold.

The islands are no longer called Las Tortugas. The name was changed on subsequent charts to indicate that the islands bore no freshwater, and thus they became the Dry Tortugas. However, more than the name has changed since Ponce de León first charted these islands. This is due largely to their geology. Unlike their counterparts in the northern section of the Keys, these islands have a more sandy composition.

The Tortugas exist in a somewhat constant state of evolutionary flux. As such, maps detailing them have changed over the years. George Gauld, a Scottish surveyor commissioned to map Florida's waters, was the first to individually name the islands on his 1775 chart. Gauld identified ten islands: Booby, East Kay, Bush Kay, Middle Kay, Logger Head Turtle Kay, Rocky Kay, Bird Kay, North Kay, Sandy Kay, and South West Kay.

Since then, however, some of those islands have disappeared. The names, too, have changed. In fact, modern charts show the Dry Tortugas as a collection of only seven islands. The islands Gauld identified as North, Sandy, and South West Kays were eroded back into the sea by hurricanes. Bird Key, once called Booby Kay, was also blown asunder by a hurricane in the 1930s. Bird Key Harbor and Bird Key Bank are still marked on modern charts.

The island Gauld first called Bird Kay is now called Middle Key. Middle Key displays the most flux, as this sandy gash of an island comes and goes, disappearing and then reforming depending on the time of year. At the other end of the spectrum, Loggerhead Key, at 30 acres, is the largest of the Tortugas. Called Logger Head Turtle Kay on Gauld's 1775 chart, the island is home to the second of the Tortugas' two lighthouses. The Loggerhead Key Lighthouse, built in 1856, is a black-and-white masonry structure standing like a 150-foot exclamation mark against the blue Atlantic horizon.

The first lighthouse in the Tortugas was built in 1825. Because that structure was eventually deemed too short and dim to adequately light such a treacherous stretch of water, the lighthouse on Loggerhead Key was constructed.

The first lighthouse was constructed on Garden Key, though J. W. Norie notes in his *Sailing Directions for the Gulf of Florida, the Bahama Bank and Islands* (1860) that he had read of a lighthouse described in an 1826 publication that was built on Garden Kay and wrote in his guide, "There is not any kay of this name in Mr. Gauld's survey of the Tortugas; it may probably be the same that he called Bush Kay."

The lighthouse indeed stands on Garden Key, the second largest of the Tortugas. But it is not the only structure built on this remote island. Garden Key is most famous as the home of Fort Jefferson, the largest completely brick structure in North America. The fort was originally designed to protect the shipping lanes between New Orleans and New York. Work began on the fort shortly after U.S. Army lieutenant Horatio Wright first landed on the Tortugas in 1846.

When the walls were completed, they encompassed 11 of Garden Key's 16 total acres. The variegated brick walls rose 45 feet up from the middle of nowhere. It took approximately 16 million bricks to build as much of the fort as they did. Most of the backbreaking work was done by slaves rented out by their Key West owners for twenty dollars a month. While hundreds of cannons fortified the walls, the interior was cultivated with rich topsoil and a soft emerald mat of Bermuda grass.

The fort was never actually completed, nor did it see any real Civil War action. The most it did was act as a Union prison for deserters, Confederates, and their sympathizers—the most famous of whom was Dr. Samuel Mudd, the doctor so infamous that he allegedly spawned the disparaging retort: "*Your name is mud!*" This is untrue, however—the saying had been in fashion before President Lincoln was assassinated.

After John Wilkes Booth shot President Lincoln behind the ear with his little gun, he jumped from the balcony at Ford's Theater and broke his leg. Mudd was the good doctor who treated the assassin's leg and then let him rest for a few hours. Mudd was caught, charged with aiding and abetting a known felon, and sentenced to Fort Jefferson along with four other alleged coconspirators.

Samuel Arnold, one of the sentenced men, kept a diary while imprisoned at the fort. A copy of an excerpt can be found at the Islamorada Branch of the Monroe County Library which reads, "Without exception, it was the most horrible place the eye of man ever rested upon, where day after day the miserable existence was being dragged out, intermixed with sickness, bodily suffering, want and pinching hunger, without the additional acts of torture and inhumanity that soon I became a witness of."

Part of the misery at the fort and around the island was mosquitoes. Mosquito netting was at a premium, and not everyone had it—certainly not the prisoners. Along with the tropical heat, mosquitoes were a harsh, painful reality. They also transmitted a potentially fatal tropical malady called yellow fever.

It struck in two waves, with initial symptoms including fever, headaches, and chills. This was followed by a short remission, but when the disease rebooted, symptoms included high fevers, intense headaches, and hemorrhaging from the nose and gums. The condition was also accompanied by jaundice and bloody vomit.

Fort Jefferson was hit hard. The fort doctor, Joseph Smith, succumbed to the disease. It is fortunate that Dr. Mudd had been incarcerated at the time of the epidemic. He filled in, treating both soldiers and prisoners alike. He, too, became infected with the disease, but Mudd made a full recovery. The good doctor was credited with saving lives and ultimately pardoned by President Andrew Johnson. Dr. Mudd was released from the prison fortress on March 8, 1869.

Life at the fort, for prisoners and soldiers alike, was one of isolation. Soldiers were not permitted alcohol at the fort, and the two great distractions for soldiers were fishing and seashell collecting. The seashells were cleaned, polished, and shipped home.

Of course, different degrees of isolation were experienced at the fort, as is revealed by diary entries from men of the 47th Regiment of Pennsylvania Veterans Volunteers who served at the fort from

December 15, 1862, to March 2, 1864. Passages reveal a rustic tapestry of prisoners, soldiers, and fort workers, as well as a number of families that called the fort home, "with 12 or 15 respectable ladies. Balls and parties are held regularly at the officers' quarters."

Another account of socialization was recorded in a letter written by an unidentified woman. "We took three boats, with music for dancing and supper, making a grand frolic of the occasion. After supper, enjoyed in the lighthouse living room, the ample kitchen was converted into a ballroom and dancing indulged until it was time for the turtles to come up."

One of the prisoners at the fort was a man named McClune, who, though incarcerated, wrote eloquently in his diary. "It is pleasant to climb to the top of the fort on a calm, clear day, and take a view of the surrounding scenery. Away in the distance the reefs are bordered by the dark-blue ocean. As the water decreases in depth it changes to an azure blue."

As for the other islands in the bunch, what is today called Bush Key lies closest to Garden Key. The two islands are sometimes separated by a narrow channel, which opens and closes periodically. Next to Bush Key is Long Key. These two are practically connected, and both are rookeries for brown noddies, masked boobies, sooty terns, and gaggles of gulls, pelicans, and egrets.

The second to last of the islands is East Key, which measures 12 acres. A soldier stationed at Fort Jefferson, Warren L. Stebbins, a private in the 110th New York Volunteers, mentioned East Key in a letter he wrote home on April 16, 1864: "Last night there was a soldier of the 110th died. His name was Evarts of Co. H. He is the 7th of the Regt. that has died since the Regt. came here. None of the soldiers hat [sic] die here on the Island are buried here but are taken to an island east here about six miles called East Keye."

The final key in the Dry Tortugas chain is Sand Key, which is not much more than a sliver of beach. The island has another name: because it was used as an isolation ward during the yellow fever epidemic of 1867, the island became known as Hospital Key. By 1875, the island was showing up on charts as Hospital Key. Like East Key, bodies were buried on it, but those old bones were unearthed years ago and washed away by the combined efforts of time, tide, and hurricanes.

In any event, the fort ended its days as a prison in 1874, and not long after, the troops were recalled from their isolated post. In a story printed by the *New York Independent* on June 2, 1882, Kirk Munroe ventured to the Tortugas, where he met an Indian living on Garden Key. The Chief, as the man was referred to, had been aboard a schooner bound for New Orleans when he was shipwrecked in the Tortugas.

"Here the Indian has remained, reveling in the delightful climate and finding it easy to supply his simple wants by wrecking, fishing, and gathering coral for Northern curiosity dealers. His cabin, just without the great gate of the fort, is built of timbers gathered from many a wreck and in and about it are quaint wooden statues that once served as figure-heads for gallant ships."

In 1888, the fort was formally turned over to the Marine Hospital Service, and for a time the structure was used as an isolation ward. Twenty years later, in 1908, the islands were declared a wildlife refuge, in part to protect nesting sooty terns. On January 4, 1935, President Franklin D. Roosevelt traveled by boat to the Tortugas and declared them a National Monument.

The monument was designated Dry Tortugas National Park in 1992. Because the Tortugas represent the very end of the archipelago, the Keys' true southernmost destination, it might seem like a hard place to get to. But it is not. If there is one thing Key West and the Florida Keys—in fact the whole of the Sunshine State—do well, it is show off their assets. Charter boats setting course for the Tortugas depart Schooner Wharf and surrounding marinas daily, weather permitting.

The prime destination of the charter trade is always Garden Key, where the snorkeling right from the beach is nothing short of fantastic. Snorkeling, however, is not the only reason to make the trip to Dry Tortugas National Park. For anyone visiting Key West, it is a brilliant excursion, and it makes for an excellent escape from cell phones. Camping sites are available for those who make reservations.

Tours of Fort Jefferson will not only afford a unique glimpse into history, but provide numerous photographic opportunities of the fascinating architecture. The Dry Tortugas are not solely sublime snorkeling fare, but also a top North American bird-watching destination.

At a Glance

Name: Dry Tortugas National Park
GPS: 24 37.27N/ 82 56.58W
Web site: www.nps.gov/drto
How to get there: The Dry Tortugas are found 70 miles southwest of Key West. There are two ways to get there: boat and plane. In either case, Garden Key, home to Fort Jefferson, is the island most visited by the local charter trade. For those taking one of the ferries departing out of the historic Schooner Wharf Seaport, expect an all-day affair. For those travelers inclined to suffer through boat rides, prepare a motion sickness strategy. Seaplane service is also offered out to these islands.

A side trip to the Garden Key excursion is the wreck of the *Avanti* (GPS: 24 37.41N/82 56.54W). This iron-hulled, three-masted Norwegian sailing ship was built in 1875. Sometimes it is referred to as the Windjammer Wreck or French Wreck. The 260-foot vessel with a beam of 40 feet was carrying lumber from Pensacola to Uruguay when it crashed on Loggerhead Reef on January 22, 1907.

It sank in 18 feet of water. Part of the ship, a very small part, breaks the surface of the ocean at low tide. Most of what is left below the surface has become encrusted with intricately designed hard corals and feathery, purple soft corals. The wreck is also home to the occasional goliath grouper.

SNORKELING SITES

Reefs

Garden Key: GPS: 24 37.469N/ 82 52.295W

Shipwrecks

Avanti: GPS: 24 37.413N/ 82 56.548W

Fun Facts

A coral polyp is generally small, in most cases smaller than a pencil eraser. It would take a great many pencil erasers, placed side by side, to become visible from outer space. Coral reefs, however, are the only living organism on this planet visible from outer space.

Acknowledgments

Thank you to David Goodhue, David Hawkins, and Karen Quist of the Florida Keys newspapers, the *Reporter* and the *Keynoter*. Thanks to Tom Hambright at the Key West Branch of the Monroe County Public Library and Kathy Ebert and Osvaldo Dominguez at the Islamorada Branch. Also to the wonderful women at University Press of Florida: Amy Gorelick, who serendipitously altered my career, Shannon McCarthy, who answers all my questions, Meredith Morris-Babb, who is always in my corner, and Sian Hunter, an excellent editor. I'd like to thank Rich McKee and Martha Otis, who give great feedback on a monthly basis, and Laura Albritton, the best writer I know. My thanks for the tireless research of my mentor, Jerry Wilkinson, as well as John Viele and Jim Clupper. Thanks to Milliard McCleary and Peter Anderson of Reef Relief, Colin Treager of the HMS Looe Foundation, and Monay Markey, public service specialist at Bahia Honda State Park. Thanks to fan number 3, my family, and my beautiful and patient wife, Michelle.

Photo Credits

Florida Keys National Marine Sanctuary: color plate pages 1–2 (all).

Jeff Anderson, Florida Keys National Marine Sanctuary: page 22.

Brad Bertelli: page 99; color plate page 8 (top).

Bill Brecht, Florida Keys National Marine Sanctuary: pages 58 and 117.

John Brooks, National Park Service: page 2.

Florida Keys National Marine Sanctuary: page 41.

Tim Grollimund: color plate pages 3–7 (all) and color plate page 8 (bottom).

Krissy Gustinger: pages 48, 112, and 115.

Todd Hitchins, Florida Keys National Marine Sanctuary: page 87.

National Oceanic Atmospheric Administration: pages ix and x.

National Park Service: page 124.

Jerry Wilkinson Collection: pages 6, 10, 18, 29, 31, 39, 40, 53, 54, 61, 64, 73, 75, 79, 93, 99, and 126.

Bibliography

Agassiz, Louis. "Report on the Florida Reefs." Memoirs of the Museum of Comparative Zoology at Harvard College 7, no. 1 (1880): plate 21.

Baker, Carlos, ed. *Ernest Hemingway: Selected Letters, 1917–1961.* New York: Scribner, 1981.

Barnes, Jay. *Florida's Hurricane History.* Chapel Hill: University of North Carolina Press, 1998.

Brookfield, Charles M. "Key Largo Coral Reef: America's First Undersea Park." *National Geographic,* Jan. 1962.

Dean, Love. *Lighthouses of the Florida Keys.* Sarasota: Pineapple Press, 1998.

Doughty, Marjorie. "Life on the Light." *Free Press,* 19 July 2000.

Enoch, Lewis, and Samuel Rhoads. *Friends' Review: A Religious, Literary, and Miscellaneous Journal* 3 (1850): 108.

Gauld, George. *Observations of the Florida Kays, Reef and Gulf; with Directions for Sailing Along the Kays, from Jamaica by the Grand Cayman and the West End of Cuba: also a description, with sailing instructions, of the coast of west Florida between the Bay of Spiritu Santo and Cape Sable.* London: W. Faden, 1796.

Gerdes, F. H. *Reconnaissance of the Florida Reef and all the Keys.* U.S. Coast Survey, 1849.

Goodrich, Caspar F. "Our Navy and the West Indian Pirates: A Documentary History, Part 3." *Proceedings Magazine* 42.12, no. 166 (1916).

Griswold, Oliver. *The Florida Keys and the Coral Reef, Authentic History of the Romantic Southernmost United State . . . From Earliest Indians to the Pennekamp Coral Reef State Park*. Miami: Graywood Press, 1965.

Grunwald, Michael. *The Swamp, The Everglades, Florida, and the Politics of Paradise*. New York: Simon & Schuster, 2006.

Holder, J. B. "Along the Florida Reef." *Harper's New Monthly Magazine* 42 (Dec. 1870–May 1871): 355–63.

Jones, Douglas, E. "Doctor Koch and His 'Immense Antediluvian Monsters.'" *Alabama Heritage* 12 (Spring 1989): 2–19.

Judson, E.Z.C. "Sketches of the Florida War—Indian Key—Its Rise, Progress and Destruction." *Western Literary Journal and Monthly Review in Pensacola Gazette* (Mar. 29, 1845).

Konstam, Angus, and Roger Michael Kean. *Pirates—Predators of the Sea: An Illustrated History*. New York: Skyhorse Publishing, 2007.

Langley, Wright, and Joan Langley. *Key West and the Spanish-American War*. Key West: Langley Press, 1998.

Macgregor, John. *The Progress of America from the Discovery by Columbus to the Year of 1846*. London: Whittaker & Co., 1847.

McCarthy, Kevin M. *Thirty Florida Shipwrecks*. Sarasota: Pineapple Press, 1992.

———. *Twenty Florida Pirates*. Sarasota: Pineapple Press, 1994.

Munroe, Kirk. "Lights of the Florida Reef." In *The Florida Adventures of Kirk Munroe*, ed. Irving A. Leonard. Chuluota, Fla.: Mickler House, 1975.

Norie, John William. *Sailing Directions for the Gulf of Florida, the Bahama Bank and Islands, and the Adjacent Coast of Cuba, and the Various Channels to New Providence*. London: Charles Wilson, 1860.

Reid, Thomas. *America's Fortress: A History of Fort Jefferson, Dry Tortugas, Florida*. Gainesville: University Press of Florida, 2006.

Scott, Thomas A. *Histories and Mysteries: The Shipwrecks of Key Largo*. Flagstaff, Ariz.: Best Publishing, 1992.

Singer, Steven D. *Shipwrecks of Florida: A Comprehensive Listing*. Sarasota: Pineapple Press, 1992.

Taylor, Thomas W. *Lore of the Reef Lights: Life in the Florida Keys*. West Conshohocken, Penn.: Infinity, 2006.

U.S. Light-House Board. "Compilation of Public Documents and Extracts from Reports and Papers, United States Bureau of Light-Houses." Washington, D.C.: Government Printing Office, 1871.

Viele, John. *The Florida Keys, Volume 1: A History of the Pioneers*. Sarasota: Pineapple Press, 1996.

———. *The Florida Keys, Volume 2: True Stories of the Perilous Straits*. Sarasota: Pineapple Press, 1999.

———. *The Florida Keys, Volume 3: The Wreckers*. Sarasota: Pineapple Press, 2001.

Weller, Bob F. *Famous Shipwrecks of the Florida Keys*. Birmingham, Ala.: EBSCO Media, 1990.

Williams, John Lee. *The Territory of Florida: Or, Sketches Of The Topography, Civil And Natural History, Of The Country, The Climate, And The Indian Tribes, From The First Discovery To The Present Time, With a Map, Views, & C.* New York: A. T. Goodrich, 1837.

Williams, Joy. *The Florida Keys: A History and Guide*. New York: Random House, 1987.

Index

Alicia, 4, 7–9

Allen, William H., 61

Alligator, U.S. schooner, 61

Alligator Lighthouse, 63–66, 77

Alligator Reef, 60–68

Amulet, 45

Anderson, Peter, 122

Anna Maria, 62–63, 66

Anne's Revenge, 11

Anniversary Reef, 8

Arnold, Samuel, 129

Arratoon Apcar, 4, 9

Atkins, Judge Clyde, 121

Avanti, 132–33

Bache Shoal, 8

Ball Buoy Reef, 3, 8

Barracudas, 60, 68

Barragan, Don Alonso Herrera, 83

Bahia Honda Bridge, 101

Bahia Honda State Park, 97–106

Beach, Dr. (Stephen Leatherman), 106

Benchly, Peter, 110

Ben Cushing, 46

Bermuda Triangle, 14

Betsy, hurricane, 30

Bibb, Edward, 14

Billander Betty, 108

Billberry, George R., 65

Bird Key, 127

Biscayne National Park, 1–12

Blackbeard, 9

Black Caesar, 9–12

Black Caesar's Rock, 9

Booth, John Wilkes, 128

Brahn, William Gerard de, 98

Brookfield, Charles M., 20, 24

Bud and Mary's Marina, 67

Buntline, Ted, 81

Bureau of Lighthouses, 65–66

Bush Key, 130

Cabbage Tree Island, 100

Caesar, lightship, 16–17

Caesar Creek, 9

Camp Bell, 78

Caribbean monk seal, 125

Carysfort, HMS, 16, 45

Carysfort Lighthouse, 20

Carysfort Reef, 13–24, 30, 32, 45

Cay Comfort, 71

Cayo Sombrero, 91

Checca Rocks, 67–68

Chekika, Chief, 76, 81

Christ of the Deep, 30
City of Washington, 33, 36–43
Cleaning stations, 96
Cleveland, President Grover, 38
Clinton Square, 121
Clupper, Jim, 65
Cody, Buffalo Bill, 81
Coffins Patch Reef, 82–89, 91
Collins, Leroy, 26–27
Collins Patches Reef, 85
Colony, 85
Conch Republic, 121
Cook, Alva, 104
Coral bleaching, 43
Coral Reef Reserve, 27, 30
Crane, Radford, 28–29
Cressi, Egidi, 30

Dale, John M., 62–63
Dennis the Menace, 34
Deodueus, 46
Discovery, 32, 34
Dog Beach, 114
Donna, hurricane, 94
Doughty, Marjorie, 21
Dry Bank, 86, 91
Dry Tortugas National Park, 123–33
Dunkirk, HMS, 14–15
Dyer, Skeeter, 120

East Key, 130
El Africa, 84
Elbow, The, 88
Elbow Reef, 33, 35, 41–42
El Floridano, 84
Elkhorn Reef, 9
Elliot Key, 11
El Rubi, 83
Emerald Reef, 9
Emma Sophia, 4

Energus, 46
Erl King, 4, 9
Everglades National Park, 26

Flagler, Henry, 101
Fletcher, Silas, 72–73
Flirt, U.S. schooner, 76
Florida, lightship, 17
Florida Board of Park and Historic
    Memorials, 104
Florida Keys Kayak, 80
Florida Patrol, 74
Florida Squadron, 75
Fort Jefferson, 123
Fort Paulding, 74–75
Forward, U.S. schooner, 93
Founders Park, 50
French Reef, 33, 45–46

Galletti, Guido, 30
Garden Key, 123, 128, 133
Gauld, George, 98, 127
Gerdes, F. H., 9, 63, 100
Goodrich, Caspar F., 4
Goodyear, Charles, 77
Goodyear Tires, 77
Great Labor Day Hurricane, 78, 101
Grecian Rocks, 32–33
Guantanamo Bay, 40
Guerrero, 17

Happy Cat, 67
Hardee, Ellison, 28
Harper's Magazine, 77
Harry Harris Park, 27, 58
Havana Harbor, 83
Hemingway, Ernest, 78
Higgs Beach, 114, 116
Holder, Dr. J. B., 77
Holm, Carl, 12

Horseshoe Reef, 33
Hospital Key, 131
Housman, John Jacob, 54–56, 71
Hudson, Harold, 21
Hydragus sillimani, 56

Indian Key, 55, 63, 69–81
Indian Key Historic State Park, 78
Islamorada, 60

John D. Pennekamp Coral Reef State
    Park, 13, 25–34, 44
Johnson, President Andrew, 129
Judson, Edward Zane Carroll, 80

Ketcham, Hank, 34
Key Largo Dry Rocks, 30, 33
Keynoter, 94
Key West, 71–72, 74, 76
Key West Admiralty Court, 53
Key West Marine Park, 114–22
Koch, Albert, 56

Last Chance Saloon, 120
Light House Board, 63, 86
Lighthouses: Alligator Lighthouse,
    63–66, 77; Carysfort Lighthouse,
    20; Loggerhead Key Lighthouse,
    127; Pacific Reef Light, 50; Som-
    brero Key Lighthouse, 85, 92
Linnard, Thomas B., 20
Loggerhead Beach, 106
Loggerhead Key, 127
Loggerhead Key Lighthouse, 127
Long Key, 130
Long Reef, 9
Looe, HMS, 108
Looe Key, 107–13
Looe Key Underwater Music Festival,
    112

Louisiana, 93–94
Lower Keys Chamber of Commerce,
    113
Lugano, 4, 9

Maine, USS, 38–40
Maitland, 21
Maloney, Walter C., 77
Mandalay, 3, 9
Maritime Heritage Trail, 3
Martí, José, 37
Marvin, Judge, 53
Mary and John Spottswood Park, 114
Maynard, Robert, 11
McKinley, President William, 38
McLaughlin, John, 75–76
Meade, George, 20, 92
Merrit and Chapman Derrick Wreck-
    ing Company, 94
Miami Herald, 26, 28
Middle Key, 127
Molasses Reef, 30, 32–33, 44–50
Mosquito Fleet, 5
Mudd, Samuel, 128
Munroe, Kirk, 14, 65, 131

Newark, 56
New Spain Fleet, 83
Nimble, 17
Norie, J. W., 99, 127
North Carolina, 55
North Dry Rocks, 33
Northhampton, 46
North North Dry Rocks, 33

Ocracoke Island, 11
Old Rhodes Key, 11
Othello, 85
Oversea Highway, 103
Oversea Railway, 100–101

Oversea Road and Toll Bridge District, 103
Oxford, 46

Pacific Reef, 9, 48
Pacific Reef Light, 50
Parks: Bahia Honda State Park, 97–106; Biscayne National Park, 1–12; Dry Tortugas National Park, 123–33; Everglades National Park, 26; Founders Park, 50; Harry Harris Park, 27, 58; Indian Key Historic State Park, 78; John D. Pennekamp Coral Reef State Park, 13, 25–34, 44; Key West Marine Park, 114–22; Mary and John Spottswood Park, 114
Parrotfish, 59
Pennekamp, John D., 26–29, 88
Pickle Barrel Wreck, 52, 57
Pickles Reef, 45, 51–59
Pilar, 78
Pillar Patch Reef, 88
Pirates, 4
Ponce de León, Juan, 83, 124
Porter, Commodore David, 5
Porter, David D., 19
Presidential Reorganization Act, 20, 65, 94
Presidents: Grover Cleveland, 38; Andrew Johnson, 129; William McKinley, 38; Franklin D. Roosevelt, 131; Harry S. Truman, 26
Proimosm, Michael, 118

Quirolo, Craig, 118
Quirolo, Devon, 118

R20 Reef, 88
Reef Relief, 118
Reefs: Alligator Reef, 60–68; Anniversary Reef, 8; Bache Shoal, 8; Ball Buoy Reef, 3, 8; Carysfort Reef, 13–24, 30, 32–33, 45; Checca Rocks, 67–68; Coffins Patch Reef, 82–89, 91; Elbow Reef, 33, 35, 41–42; Elkhorn Reef, 9; Emerald Reef, 9; French Reef, 33, 45–46; Grecian Rocks, 32–33; Horseshoe Reef, 33; Key Largo Dry Rocks, 30, 33; Long Reef, 9; Molasses Reef, 30, 32–33, 44–50; North Dry Rocks, 33; North North Dry Rocks, 33; Pacific Reef, 9, 48; Pickles Reef, 45, 51–59; Pillar Patch Reef, 88; R20 Reef, 88; Sand Circle Reef, 88; Sombrero Reef, 86, 90–96; The Stake, 86, 88; Triumph Reef, 9; Turtle Reef, 33
Revenge, 62
Reynolds Avenue, 116
Richards, Richard C., 66
Roach's Shipyard, 36
Robbies Marina, 67, 80
Romans, Bernard, 71
Roosevelt, President Franklin D., 131

San Carlos Institute, 37
Sand Circle Reef, 88
Sand Key, 130
Sandspur Beach, 106
Sandwich Cove, 1
San Ignacio, 84
San Pedro Underwater Archaeological and State Preserve, 89
Schooner Wharf Bar, 122
Second Seminole War, 19, 73
Seminole Street, 114
Shark Reef, 9
Sharks, 110
Shaw, Donna, 30
Shaw, Herbert, 30
Shipwrecks: Alicia 4, 7–9; Alligator,

61; *Amulet*, 45; *Arratoon Apcar*, 4, 9; *Avanti*, 132–33; *Ben Cushing*, 46; HMS *Carysfort*, 16, 45; *City of Washington*, 33, 36–43; *Colony*, 85; *Deodueus*, 46; *El Africa*, 84; *El Floridano*, 84; *El Rubi*, 83; *Energus*, 46; *Erl King*, 4, 9; *Guerrero*, 17; HMS *Looe*, 108; *Louisiana*, 93–94; *Lugano*, 4, 9; *Maitland*, 21; *Mandalay*, 3, 9; *Northhampton*, 46; *Othello*, 85; *Oxford*, 46; Pickle Barrel Wreck, 52, 57; San Pedro Underwater Archaeological and State Preserve, 89; *San Ignacio*, 84; *Slabdova*, 46; *Slabodna*, 47; *Wellwood*, 49; HMS *Winchester*, 14–16, 23–24; *Yucatan*, 45
Singer, Steven D., 46
Slabdova, 46
Slabodna, 47
Smith, Joseph, 129
Sombrero Key Lighthouse, 85, 92
Sombrero Reef, 86, 90–96
Soule, John, 15
South Beach, 114
Spanish American War, 40
Stake, The, 86, 88
Stansbury, Captain Howard, 19
Stebbins, Warren L., 130

Tarracino, Captain Tony, 122
Taylor, Frank, 21
Teach, Edwards, 11
Tea Table Fill, 80
Tea Table Key, 74
Totten, James, 85, 92
Triumph Reef, 9
Tropical Hotel, 74
Truman, President Harry S., 26

Turtle Harbor, 16
Turtle Reef, 33
Turtles, 125

Underwater Society of America, 30
United States Post Office Indian Key Station, 73
Upper Matecumbe Key, 67
Utting, Captain, 108

Vera Cruz, Mexico, 83
Vernon Street, 114
Voss, Gilbert, 27

Wardlow, Dennis, 121
Webb, Judge, 53, 56
Wellwood, 49
West Indies Squadron, 61
Whalton, John, 16–19
White Street Pier, 114
Wilkinson, Jerry, 77
William Henry, 71
Williams, John Lee, 91, 100
Williams, Joy, 87
Williamson, Furman C., 94
Winchester, HMS, 14–16, 23–24
Winch Hole, 46–47
Worthington, Evalena, 122
Worthington, Paul, 122
Wreckers, 7, 52–57
Wright, Horacio, 128

Yellow fever, 129
Yucatan, 45

Zeuglodon, 57
Zooxanthellae, 43, 59

Brad Bertelli is an award-winning writer and member of the Florida Outdoor Writers Association. He is currently the vice president of the Historical Preservation Society of the Upper Keys. Author of *Snorkeling Florida: 50 Excellent Sites*, Brad has also written articles for the *Miami Herald* as well as the Florida Keys newspapers, the *Reporter* and the *Keynoter*. A snorkeling enthusiast and historian, Brad lives in Islamorada with his wife, Michelle.

The University Press of Florida is the scholarly publishing agency for the State University System of Florida, comprising Florida A&M University, Florida Atlantic University, Florida Gulf Coast University, Florida International University, Florida State University, New College of Florida, University of Central Florida, University of Florida, University of North Florida, University of South Florida, and University of West Florida.